Experiments in the Social Sciences

First published 1975

Published by Harper & Row Ltd.
28 Tavistock Street, London WC2E 7PN

Standard Book Number 06-318014-6

Designed by Millions
Typeset by Preface Ltd, Salisbury, Wiltshire
Printed and bound by the Garden City Press,
Letchworth, Hertfordshire

Experiments in the Social Sciences

GEOFFREY BROWN, MEd., PhD

DEREK H. CHERRINGTON, DCP, MEd

LOUIS COHEN, MA, MEd., PhD

Harper & Row, Publishers

London   New York   Evanston   San Francisco

ACKNOWLEDGEMENTS

533574

Students in the following colleges for their valuable assistance in testing the various experiments: Anstey College of Physical Education, Sutton Coldfield: Bingley College of Education, Bingley: City of Sheffield College of Education: Ilkley College of Education, Ilkley: Leeds and Carnegie College of Education, Leeds: Margaret McMillan College of Education, Bradford: St Martin's College of Education, Lancaster: Trinity and All Saints College of Education, Horsforth, Leeds.

Full-time and part-time students following the Advanced Diploma in the Psychology and Sociology of Education, and the MSc. (Education) degree at the School of Research in Education, University of Bradford.

Eddie Altman, MEd., Principal Lecturer in Education, Bingley College of Education, Bingley. Derek Bagshaw, MSc., Senior Lecturer in Education, Ilkley College of Education, Ilkley. Kenneth Boothroyd, MA, MSc., Senior Lecturer in Education, Huddersfield Polytechnic, Huddersfield. Brian Hopkins, MS, formerly Research Assistant, Anstey College of Physical Education, Sutton Coldfield. Peter Jennings, Senior Lecturer in Education, St. Martin's College of Education, Lancaster. James Keegan, MSc., Principal Lecturer in Communications Media, Trinity and All Saints College of Education, Horsforth, Leeds. Lawrence Manion, BA, MusB, MSc., PhD, Principal Lecturer in Music, Didsbury College of Education, for permission to use the Self-Identity Questionnaire (College form) in Experiment 7. J. Brown and Occupational Psychology for Tables A2:7 and A2:8.

F. W. Kellaway and Penguin for permission to reproduce Tables A2:10, A2:11, A2:12 and A2:13. Albert Mehrabian, University of Los Angeles, for permission to use the Achievement Orientation Measure in Experiment 19. A. N. Oppenheim and Heinemann for permission to reproduce Figures A2:1, A2:2 and A2:3. Milton Rokeach, University of Washington, for permission to use the Value Survey Instrument in Experiment 8. S. S. Siegel and McGraw-Hill for permission to reproduce Tables A2:1, A2:5 and A2:14.

CONTENTS

Psychology and sociology belong to a group of related disciplines referred to as the social sciences. Much controversy has arisen from attempts to define what the term 'science' implies, and whether these disciplines can appropriately be classed as similar to the natural sciences such as physics and chemistry. The authors do not intend to join that controversy in this book. Their intention is to show that experimental methods designed for research in the social sciences can be usefully incorporated into academic courses in just the same way that teachers of natural sciences incorporate practical work into their syllabuses. The advantages of such action are many: students increasingly feel that the phenomena they are studying are real, they understand the phenomena better, begin to get a sense of the way in which research is carried out, become less scared of statistics, and perhaps more crucially, find the work enjoyable.

This book is not a course text. It is a valuable complement to any of the standard texts used in teaching social sciences to sixth form students, students in colleges of education and colleges of further education, and in polytechnics and universities. It contains experiments covering major features of most syllabuses in psychology and sociology. These may be selected by the course tutor and introduced at appropriate times.

One major difference between this and other books currently available is that here the experiments are designed for use in classroom situations, and the majority can be used with relatively small classes of 16 to 20 students. In addition, the experiments do not require sophisticated laboratory equipment, nor do they demand a high level of mathematical skill. All the experiments have been thoroughly tested, the specimen data are real data from groups of students the authors have taught. To all those students the authors gratefully acknowledge their debt.

HOW TO USE THIS BOOK

Each experiment is in two sections: The first is intended for the teacher/organizer and those people in the group who are not acting as subjects. It gives details of how the experiment should be conducted and how it should be analysed. Subjects should be instructed to consult this section only after the experiment has been performed. The section at the end of the book on coloured pages gives sufficient information for members of the group who will act as subjects. It avoids giving any information which might influence the ways in which they will react.

Each experiment has a summary and is accompanied by references to sources of the procedure, i.e. these are 'technical references'. **Groups of experiments** are related to a central theme, and each is expanded in an overview which is accompanied by 'general references' which are more adily accessible to students.

In everyday life people are constantly making judgments about the type of people they are in contact with, about the chances of it raining that day, about the way in which they should tackle a problem, and about hundreds of other things which confront them. To make these judgments they often rely upon what they hold to be the *common sense* view. There is a problem, however, because the individual may have no means of ascertaining that his view is really 'common' to all, or even many, people. Whilst seeming eminently sensible to him, the view may be totally opposed to that held by other people. Even if the viewpoint is fairly widespread this is not to say that it is correct, or really 'sense'. Thus the individual's judgment, rationalized as being common sense, may be neither common nor sense to someone else. Basically, the function of research is to determine how widespread a certain phenomenon might be, and/or whether a viewpoint is correct or not.

The previous paragraph may seem somewhat pedantic. In fact we all use common sense for much of the time, and often very successfully. To demand tested hypotheses before pronouncing judgment would make life unbearable. (The story of the young barrister who responded to his child's observation: 'Daddy, look those sheep have been sheared' with the reply, 'Well, they have on this side, dear!', is probably apocryphal.) In some quarters the reader may encounter a certain suspicion of the researcher. There may be any number of reasons for this suspicion, but perhaps it helps to bear in mind that research findings do not appear from nowhere. They are the results of systematic attempts to verify observations which may have come from folk-lore, or from the intuitions of reasonable people. So researchers do not have access to some mystical and esoteric knowledge; they are often simply engaged in trying to empirically verify common sense.

There are two forms of research in the social sciences — 'field research' and formal 'experimental research'. These two methodologies are really poles of a continuum, as many studies use aspects of both, but for the sake of simplicity we shall consider them as discrete. Field studies are concerned with investigating phenomena as they exist in everyday life. An investigation of the moral standards of sixth formers would be of this type. Experimental studies, on the other hand, attempt to control and manipulate aspects of a situation in order to observe the effects. Depriving subjects of measured amounts of sleep in order to observe effects upon their intellectual powers would be an experimental study. The latter could be accomplished by surveying large sectors of the population for insomniacs, but the technical problems would be very great. (The reader might like to work out the pros and cons of these alternate methodologies.)

The survey is perhaps the most straightforward research method. It involves constructing a questionnaire or inventory and asking research fieldworkers or the subjects of the enquiry to fill it in. This perhaps passes off the effort rather too lightly. In fact, the construction of a good questionnaire is a lengthy and complicated business, and should not be undertaken without adequate guidance (see, for instance, Oppenheim 1966). The information obtained from a good questionnaire may be entirely factual, such as the number of car-owning residents in an area, or it may need some interpretation if it is seeking more elusive data such as opinions and attitudes.

Careful interpretation is also necessary in situations in which it has not been possible to survey everyone. Data obtained from National Opinion Poll (NOP) percentages and Television Audience Measurement (TAM) ratings are of this type. They are used to form generalized opinions about how the whole of the population thinks about certain events, yet the number actually questioned is often quite small. To do this it is necessary to use sampling techniques which try to ensure that the few who are asked will give views which are representative of the many. The same principle applies when persons must be allocated to certain groups for an experiment. To ask for volunteers would be very hazardous as it is unlikely that those who readily offer their assistance are the same sorts of people as those who 'hang back' and are reluctant to cooperate. A simple way of trying to prevent this is to draw the names of subjects out of a hat. This is a form of what is termed 'random sampling'.

Behaviour occurs in situations in which dozens, maybe thousands, of factors may be variable from one situation to the next. The aim of experimental method is to control as many of these as possible so that the relationships between two or three can be studied. Of course, there is a danger that the highly simplified experimental situation may be so unlike the real-life situation that the subjects respond in totally different ways. This is a criticism which must always be borne in mind when commenting upon the implications of experimental findings.

Experimental design can become very complex, with very sophisticated statistics being used to analyse the data, but here we shall restrict ourselves to relatively simple models which show all the essential features of experiments. An experiment starts with a 'hunch' or an observation which gives rise to an hypothesis which can be tested. Let us say that a student has been reading a book of very fine print. He subsequently fails to recall much of the content when questioned about it in a seminar. He concludes that recall of the content of printed matter is less when the print is fine. This conclusion is an hypothesis, and can be tested by experiment.

The formation of a hypothesis has two useful functions. Firstly, it serves to synthesize the experimenter's knowledge of previous research into a prediction which can be handled experimentally and, secondly, gives direction to his subsequent investigations. This does not imply that hypotheses are always very precise statements. Particularly in descriptive survey work the situation may be so unknown that nothing but an interest in finding out what is happening is given as a rationale. In experimental work, however, the hypothesis is usually much more precise, for it provides the means by which the variables are chosen.

The experiment we would set up to test our myopic friend's conclusion will have two variables, which can be measured. The first is the size of the print. As experimenters we can vary this, but it is independent of the student's ability to recall and is termed the *independent variable.* According to the hypothesis the quantity of material which the student can recall is dependent upon this. It is the *dependent variable.*

The student's powers of recall probably differ quite a lot from time to time, even when the size of print does not vary. So any differences in measured recall between material printed in different sizes has got to be sufficiently large to be distinguished from the random fluctuations observed. There is also the chance that our student may be a very unusual type, or may have an 'off day' when we want to do the experiment. To be more sure of our results it will be better to pick random groups of students.

So we will use two randomly-picked groups of students, and prepare one piece of prose in two forms, one in fine print and the other in large print. We will ask one group to read one form and the other group the other form. Then we will test both groups in the same way.

Table 1 Experimental Schedule for Investigating Effects of Print Size on Recall

Group	Task	Test
E_1	Small print	√
E_2	Large print	√

This still leaves some important decisions to be made. Should both task and test be timed sessions? Would that be more, or less, fair to all subjects than if they work at their own rates? Should the test be of 'recall' or 'understanding'? These are decisions which the experimenter has to make, and which he *must* report, for they affect the extent to which his results may be generalized and compared with other studies.

In any experiment which uses tests there are two recognized criteria by which the tests will be assessed. The first of these is *validity*. The validity of a test is the extent to which it measures what it purports to measure. If a test sets out to measure an individual's knowledge of the six-times multiplication table, validity is not likely to be a problem. The validity of tests of intelligence, aptitude or physical skill, however, can often only be established after intensive investigation of their relationships to other tests and other behavioural characteristics. To simply label a test is no guarantee that it is valid.

The other criterion is *reliability*. This is an estimate of the precision with which an individual's score is made. Tests which are easily affected by day to day variations in the subjects' dispositions or testers' procedures are less reliable than those which are not. In our experiment, testing 'recall' may offer less problems than testing 'understanding', but would the findings be as useful?

If the reader is asked to perform this study he could probably do it quite successfully. When he had marked his tests, however, he is likely to encounter a difficult problem: 'How will I know if the differences between groups are big enough?' If all the E_2 subjects scored 15 out of 20, or better, and all the E_1 subjects scored five or less, we need hardly be concerned. However, such clear-cut results are very rare. It was also observed earlier that performances tend to fluctuate anyway, so we need to know what fluctuations we can 'put down to chance', and what fluctuations are likely to indicate real differences due to print size. This is essentially what the statistical test tells us. Whatever test we use we shall arrive at a value which indicates a *level of confidence*. This means, quite literally, the confidence we can have that our differences between groups are not due to chance.

Assume that we have tested Groups E_1 and E_2 (Table 1), and that the scores are tested by a procedure which indicates a difference between groups at the 5 per cent level (often written $p < 0.05$). This tells us that there are only five chances in every 100 that such differences between E_1 and E_2 groups would occur by chance. A social scientist would usually accept this as confirming a real difference, though he may be happier with $p < 0.01$ (i.e. only one chance in 100) or $p < 0.001$ (only one chance in 1,000). If he found $p < 0.5$ this would mean that there was a 50–50 chance that differences of that size could occur quite by chance, even if E_1 and E_2 had read the same print. Thus, the hypothesis would be rejected.

In brief, one may say that the experiment must be designed in such a way that, if the data confirms our hypothesis, it must confirm only our hypothesis and not several others too.

One vital feature of research we tend to take for granted is the report. Occasionally there is a major 'breakthrough' in a research area, but by far the greater part of the progress in knowledge is achieved by a slow build-up of information from many research studies of quite modest proportions. Clear research reports are essential to this process. The experiments in this book are offered as examples of the sorts of phenomena dealt with in a typical course, but it is hoped that many of the readers may subsequently want to follow their own research interests. The following summary is offered as a guide to reporting experimental work. Readers should adopt this system when writing up the experiments they have performed.

1   Title—
this should state clearly and succinctly what the experiment was about (and when it was carried out).

2   Introduction—
a synopsis of relevant previous research.

3   Aim—
a brief statement of what the experiment set out to do.

4   Method.
(a)   The number and type of subjects, and how they were selected.

(b)   The materials used.

(c)   How the experiment was conducted.

5   Results.
(a)   How scoring was accomplished and how the raw scores were obtained.

(b)   How the raw scores were analysed.

6   Discussion—
how were the results interpreted and what were the limitations of the design and procedures?

7   Conclusion—
what conclusions may be drawn from this experiment and how do they relate to previous work in this area?

8   References—
there are standard methods of listing references. That used in this book is a common system. As the reader may be unfamiliar with accepted abbreviations of titles, they have been stated in full, and this system is recommended to the beginner.

14

DO NOT CONSULT THIS SECTION UNTIL TOLD TO DO SO.
PARTICIPANTS SHOULD REFER TO THE COLOURED SECTION
AT THE END.

CONFORMITY TO NORMS

Aim

To test the null* hypothesis that male drivers of private cars are not significantly different from female drivers of private cars in their conformity to the norm of stopping at a 'stop' sign.

Method

The design of the experiment follows that of Dean and Valdes (1963). Pairs of students make joint observations of behaviour at a 'stop' sign, each pair corroborates the classification of the behaviour of ten male and ten female drivers of private cars. The observations are collated and classified as follows:

Drivers	Absolute stop	Slowed but did not stop
Male		
Female		

Suggestions for conducting the experiment

The following instructions have been found useful in briefing student observers.

1   Discuss fully with all observers the exact meaning of the classifications *'absolute stop, slowed down but did not stop'*, so that they are quite clear in distinguishing between them. The paired observations are intended as a further check.

2   Use *one* 'stop' sign location for all the observations.

3   Make observations at approximately the same time of day.

4   Choose a 'stop' sign junction where traffic can be clearly seen for a reasonable distance approaching from the right-hand side.

5   Record the behaviour of only those drivers who turn *left* from the 'stop' sign.

6   Only record the behaviour of a driver at the 'stop' sign where there is no car approaching from the right which is nearer than 30 yards.

7   When two or more drivers are at the 'stop' sign at the same time, only the first driver's behaviour should be recorded.

---

*The null hypothesis is saying, in effect: 'There is no relationship between the sex of the driver and his/her conformity to the requirement to stop at a 'stop' sign — but, go ahead and disprove the proposition if you can!'
Sir Roland Fisher (1951) observes, 'Every experiment may be said to exist only in order to give the facts a chance of disproving the null hypothesis'.

Analysis

Chi-Square is a statistical technique appropriate for the analysis of the data (see Appendix 2, p. 205, Treatment 7). By way of example, 206 observations of driving behaviour in a Midlands city suburb were recorded by paired observers at one 'stop' sign. Their recordings were classified as follows:

Drivers	Absolute stop	Slowed but did not stop	Total
Male	73	72	145
Female	42	19	61
Total	115	91	206

The differences between these cells, when tested by chi-square analysis was found to be significant at the 0.05 level, i.e. $\chi^2 = 5.23$ with 1 d.f.

Summary

We may reject the null hypothesis and conclude that in the sample we have observed, male drivers are significantly less conforming than female drivers in their behaviour at a 'stop' sign.

(O)

Drivers	Absolute stop	Slowed but did not stop	Total
Male			
Female			
Total			

(E)

Male	
Female	

$(O - E)$ corrected

Male	
Female	

$$\frac{(O - E)^2}{E}$$

Male	
Female	

$$\chi^2 = \Sigma \ \frac{(O - E)^2}{E}$$

d.f. =

Interpret your findings in the above analysis and write them down briefly.

_____

_____

_____

_____

_____

Further Applications

1 Behaviour of motorists at zebra crossings, within restricted speed zones and at parking places offer further areas for observation of conformity to norms in everyday life.

2 The school provides opportunities to observe conformity to school norms in relation to running in corridors, lateness, etc.

3 The college library will have records of students whose library books are in various categories of 'overdue please return'.

4 Observations such as those suggested above, sub-classified by age or sex or class in school etc., offer interesting lines of exploration.

References

DEAN, D. G. and VALDES, D. M. Experiments in Sociology, Appleton-Century-Crofts, New York, 1963.
FISHER, R. The Design of Experiments, Hafner, New York, 6th edition, 1951.
KELVIN, P. The Bases of Social Behaviour, Holt, Rinehart and Winston, London, Chap. 3, 'Norms and Conformity', 1969.

SOCIAL CLASS STEREOTYPES

Aim

To investigate the social class stereotypes of student groups.

Method

The design of the experiment follows the Asch technique described by Jahoda in Humphrey and Argyle (1962). The subjects are given six written statements about a hypothetical Mr 'X'. In all conditions five of the statements remain the same, only the sixth statement is varied as follows:

Is 43 years old.	Is 43 years old.
Has a wife and three children.	Has a wife and three children.
Served in the forces.	Served in the forces.
Owns a large country house.	*Owns a semi-detached house.*
Enjoys pictures.	Enjoys pictures.
Is keen on sport.	Is keen on sport.

Is 43 years old.	Is 43 years old.
Has a wife and three children.	Has a wife and three children.
Served in the forces.	Served in the forces.
Lives in a council house.	*Lives in a crowded tenement.*
Enjoys pictures.	Enjoys pictures.
Is keen on sport.	Is keen on sport.

The subjects are randomly assigned to the four conditions as given on Cards 1, 2, 3 and 4. Care must be taken to ensure that subjects do not read each other's cards. Subjects are then asked to complete a personality inventory for Mr 'X', based on their impression of him.

Personality Inventory of Mr 'X'

Consider the 20 pairs of alternatives below. For each pair underline the one statement which you feel best applies to the person described on your card. If you are not sure make a guess. Do not omit any items.

1	Mainly an optimist.	Mainly a pessimist.
2	Regards his work lightly.	Conscientious in his work.
3	Spends much time with his children.	Usually leaves his children to their own devices.
4	Tends to be thrifty.	Rather reckless with money.
5	Rarely helps with the housework.	Often helps in the house.
6	Lives mainly in the present.	Plans for the future.
7	Attentive to his wife.	Apt to take his wife for granted.
8	Quite fond of gambling.	Opposed to gambling.
9	Self-reliant.	Dependent on others.
10	Somewhat untidy.	Meticulous in his habits.
11	Largely self-centred.	Great concern for others.
12	Active church member.	Not bothered about religion.
13	Loud and boisterous.	Quiet and reserved.
14	Shares his wife's interests.	He and his wife go their own ways.
15	Left in politics.	Right in politics.
16	Slow and deliberate.	Quick and impulsive.
17	Somewhat ambitious.	Has few ambitions.
18	Rather patriotic.	Not very patriotic.
19	On friendly terms with his neighbours.	Tends to remain aloof from his neighbours.
20	Scrupulously honest.	Not averse to petty dishonesty.

Categorize subjects' responses according to their cards. Total for each of the four card-groups the number of left- or right-hand underlinings on the personality inventory on each item. Enter these in Table 1:1 below.

Table 1:1

	Country house		Semi-detached		Council		Tenement	
Items	L	R	L	R	L	R	L	R
1								
2								
3								
4								
5								
6								
7								
8								
9								
10								
11								
12								
13								
14								
15								
16								
17								
18								
19								
20								

In Table 1:2 below, the responses of 94 College of Education students are categorized on each of the 20 personality items.

Table 1:2

Items	Country house		Semi-detached		Council		Tenement	
	L	R	L	R	L	R	L	R
1	23	3	24	1	21	0	13	9
2	7	19	5	20	6	15	11	11
3**	17	9	21	4	16	5	8	14
4*	13	13	19	6	10	11	7	15
5*	21	5	10	15	12	9	11	11
6**	10	16	7	18	16	5	20	2
7	15	11	16	9	12	9	8	14
8*	20	6	10	15	12	9	16	6
9	22	4	22	3	14	7	15	7
10*	12	14	9	16	6	15	16	6
11	12	14	10	15	10	11	13	9
12	8	18	10	15	4	17	2	20
13	21	5	10	15	12	9	13	9
14*	13	13	17	8	11	10	6	16
15	10	16	8	17	11	10	11	11
16*	8	18	18	7	13	8	9	13
17**	21	5	13	12	7	14	4	18
18*	22	4	19	6	17	4	11	11
19	17	9	19	6	19	2	19	3
20	15	11	15	10	11	10	13	9

*Significant at 0.05 level   **Significant at 0.01 level

Analysis

We wish to find out whether we are justified in assuming that the distribution of scores on each item in Table 1.2 above represents a real difference in subjects' beliefs or whether the distribution of scores could have occurred by chance. Chi-square is an appropriate statistic by which to compare the observed frequencies with those we might expect if we assumed chance only (see Appendix 2, Treatment 7).

Example:
Item 6   *Observed frequencies*

	Country House	Semi-Detached	Council House	Tenement	Total
Left column	10	7	16	20	53
Right column	16	18	5	2	41
Total	26	25	21	22	94

Analysis of this item by x^2 shows that there is a difference between cells which is significant at the 0.01 level ($x^2 = 25.59$ with 3 d.f.). We may therefore conclude that country house and semi-detached house dwellers tend to plan for the future whereas council house and tenement dwellers live mainly for the present.

Summary

Examining the responses of the 94 College of Education students, on ten items there are significant differences in beliefs about the occupants of the four types of residence. The directions of those differences are interpreted below.

Item 3   The country-house dweller spends much time with his children whereas the tenement dweller more often leaves them to their own devices.

Item 4   The semi-detached house-owner is thrifty whereas the tenement dweller is rather reckless with money.

Item 5   The country-house owner rarely helps with the housework whereas the semi-detached house-owner often does.

Item 6   The country-house and the semi-detached house-owners tend to plan for the future whereas the council house and tenement dwellers live mainly in the present.

Item 8   Country-house owners are fairly fond of gambling whereas semi-detached house-owners are more generally opposed to it.

Item 10   The tenement dweller is untidy whereas the semi-detached house-owner and council house dweller tend to be more meticulous in their habits.

Item 14   The semi-detached house-owner tends to share his wife's interests whereas the tenement dweller and his wife go their own ways.

Item 16   Country-house owners and tenement dwellers are quick and impulsive whereas semi-detached house-owners and council house dwellers are more slow and deliberate.

Item 17   The country-house owners are somewhat ambitious whereas tenement dwellers have few ambitions.

Item 18   Country house, semi-detached house, and council house dwellers are rather patriotic whereas tenement dwellers tend to be less so.

Card 1	**Card 2**
Is 43 years old.	Is 43 years old.
Has a wife and three children.	Has a wife and three children.
Served in the forces.	Served in the forces.
Owns a large country house.	Owns a semi-deatched house.
Enjoys pictures.	Enjoys pictures.
Is keen on sport.	Is keen on sport.
Card 3	**Card 4**
Is 43 years old.	Is 43 years old.
Has a wife and three children.	Has a wife and three children.
Served in the forces.	Served in the forces.
Lives in a council house.	Lives in a crowded tenement.
Enjoys pictures.	Enjoys pictures.
Is keen on sport.	Is keen on sport.

Personality inventory — of Mr 'X'

Consider the 20 pairs of alternatives below. For each pair underline the one statement which you feel best applies to the person described on your card. If you are not sure make a guess. Do not omit any items.

1	Mainly an optimist.	Mainly a pessimist.
2	Regards his work lightly.	Conscientious in his work.
3	Spends much time with his children.	Usually leaves his children to their own devices.
4	Tends to be thrifty.	Rather reckless with money.
5	Rarely helps with the housework.	Often helps in the house.
6	Lives mainly in the present.	Plans for the future.
7	Attentive to his wife.	Apt to take his wife for granted.
8	Quite fond of gambling.	Opposed to gambling.
9	Self-reliant.	Dependent on others.
10	Somewhat untidy.	Meticulous in his habits.
11	Largely self-centred.	Great concern for others.
12	Active church member.	Not bothered about religion.
13	Loud and boisterous.	Quiet and reserved.
14	Shares his wife's interests.	He and his wife go their own ways.
15	Left in politics.	Right in politics.
16	Slow and deliberate.	Quick and impulsive.
17	Somewhat ambitious.	Has few ambitions.
18	Rather patriotic	Not very patriotic.
19	On friendly terms with his neighbours.	Tends to remain aloof from his neighbours.
20	Scrupulously honest.	Not averse to petty dishonesty.

Categorize subjects' responses according to their cards. Total for each of the four card-groups the number of left- or right-hand underlinings on the personality inventory on each item. Enter these in Table 1:3 below.

Table 1:3

	Country house		Semi-detached		Council		Tenement	
Items	L	R	L	R	L	R	L	R
1								
2								
3								
4								
5								
6								
7								
8								
9								
10								
11								
12								
13								
14								
15								
16								
17								
18								
19								
20								

From your chi-square analysis of each item, examine the cells which contribute to any significant differences that you find. Interpret the differences item by item.

Item _____

_____

_____

Item _____

_____

_____

Item _____

_____

_____

Item _____

_____

_____

Item _____

_____

_____

Item _____

_____

_____

Item _____

_____

_____

Item _____

_____

_____

Further applications

The way in which an individual's personality is related to his social perceptions is an area that students may care to investigate. Rokeach's Dogmatism Scale (Rokeach, 1960) may be used to identify open-minded and closed-minded subjects before the analysis of their social class perceptions as in the above study. Alternatively, the Social Attitudes Inventory (Eysenck, 1954) identifying tough-minded and tender-minded individuals might be used as the independent personality variable. Examine Centers' (1961) research which asked over 1,000 people: 'What puts a person in the lower classes?'. What similarities do you note between the social perceptions of Centers' respondents and those of the subjects participating in Experiment 2?

References

CENTERS, R. The Psychology of Social Classes, Russell and Russell, p. 96, Table 25, 1961.
EYSENCK, J. H. Sense and Nonsense in Psychology, Penguin, London, 1957.
EYSENCK, H. J. The Psychology of Politics, Routledge and Kegan Paul, London, 1954.
HUMPHREY, G. and ARGYLE, M. Social Psychology Through Experiment, Methuen, London, 1962.
ROKEACH, M. The Open and Closed Mind, Basic Books Inc, New York, 1960.
TAJFEL, H. and WILKES, A. L. Judgments in the Perceptions of People, British Journal of Social and Clinical Psychology, 2, pp. 40–49, 1963.

RUMOUR

Aim:

To demonstrate the changes and distortions that occur as rumour travels. The experiment is based upon the Allport and Postman Rumour Study. A tape-recording of the experiment provides an exact account to which reference can be made when discussing sharpening, levelling and assimilation processes. The recording enables the experimenter to check audience ratings given to the subjects' versions of the story.

Method

Seven to ten volunteers are isolated from the audience which is then shown a large size, anglicized version of the original Allport and Postman picture (see p. 34). A checklist consisting of 20 items describing the picture is distributed to each member of the audience. The experimenter reads through the list of items referring where appropriate to the actual picture which remains visible to the audience throughout the experiment. The scoring of the subject-volunteers' versions of the picture is explained as follows:

1   Award two marks for a perfect or almost perfect reproduction of the original item as set out on your checklist.

2   Award one mark for a reasonably accurate reproduction of the original item as set out on your checklist.

3   Award no marks for failure to mention the item.

4   In the space at the bottom of your checklist, note any interesting additions that subjects make when re-telling the story, placing S1, S2, S3, etc., after the note to identify the person.

Procedure

1   S1 enters room and sits where he cannot see the picture.

2   Tape-recorder started.

3   Experimenter reads from checklist describing slowly and clearly the picture, having warned S1 that he will be asked to re-tell as accurately as possible to S2.

4   S2 enters room.

5   Audience markers prepare to score S1 version to S2.

6   S1 recounts story to S2.

7   S2 recounts story to S3.

8   Each subject in turn, hears and re-tells the story.

9   Checklists are collected and scores collated.

10   Total aggregate scores for each subject are plotted against successive reproductions to show levelling.

11   Total item scores across subjects' reproductions are obtained to show sharpening and dropout of details.

Analysis

Below is an analysis of the processes of change occurring when seven subjects (second-year student teachers in a college of education) took part in the rumour experiment and ten members of the student audience acted as checkers.

Results

Subjects $n = 7$ Audience checkers = ten pairs, one pair to two items

Table 1:4

items		1	2	3	4	5	6	7	8	9	10	Total score
1	The scene is a London railway station	4	4	4	4	3	4	3				26
2	The station is Paddington	4	4	4	4	0	0	0				16
3	Seven adults in the compartment	4	4	1	1	0	0	0				10
4	Five are seated	4	4	0	0	0	0	0				8
5	Two are standing	4	4	0	0	0	0	0				8
6	Two are women	4	1	0	0	0	0	0				5
7	One woman has a baby	4	4	4	3	3	4	4				26
8	A Negro is standing	4	4	4	4	3	2	1				22
9	He is well-dressed	0	0	0	0	0	0	0				0
10	A white man is standing	4	4	4	2	4	1	1				20
11	He threatens the Negro	4	4	4	0	0	0	0				12
12	The white man has an open razor	4	4	4	0	0	0	0				12
13	The woman with the baby watches anxiously	4	4	4	3	0	0	0				15
14	The other woman has a flowery hat	4	4	4	4	0	0	0				16
15	She also has a fur collar on her coat	0	0	0	0	0	0	0				0
16	A man is reading the *Daily Express*	4	2	4	4	4	4	4				26
17	Another man is asleep	0	0	0	0	0	0	0				0
18	There is a Jewish man	3	0	0	0	0	0	0				3
19	He has a book on his knee	0	0	0	0	0	0	0				0
20	There are advertisements for cigarettes, shoes, etc.	2	0	0	0	0	0	0				2
	Totals	61	51	41	29	17	15	13				

Subjects

Figure 1:1 The process of sharpening

Sharpening refers to the retention of a limited number of details from the total story. The aggregate score of all subjects on each item serves to show those details which persist during later reproductions.

Item	Score	
1	26 ——————————————	The scene is a London railway station
2	16 ——————————————	The station is Paddington
3	10	
4	8	
5	8	
6	5	
7	26 ——————————————	One woman has a baby
8	22 ——————————————	A Negro is standing
9	0	
10	20 ——————————————	A white man is standing
11	12	
12	12	
13	15	
14	16	
15	0	
16	26 ——————————————	A man is reading the *Daily Express*
17	0	
18	3	
19	0	
20	2	

Figure 1:2 The process of assimilation by contraction

Experimenter		S1
Item 17	Another man is asleep	
Item 18	There is a Jewish man	There's also a Jew — seated — the Jew is asleep
Item 19	He has a book on his knee	

Figure 1:3 Examination of item 16 to illustrate the scoring on the item and the persistence of the detail from S1 to S7

S1	A man reading the *Daily Express* (score 4)
S2*	There's a woman reading the *Daily Express* (score 2)
S3	There's a man reading the *Daily Express* (score 4)
S4	There's a man, sitting down, reading the *Daily Express* (score 4)
S5	There's a man with the *Daily Express*, sitting down (score 4)
S6	A man reading an Express paper (score 4)
S7	A man reading an Express newspaper (score 4)

*Note how after subject two's mistaken attribution of reading the newspaper to a woman (score two marks only), subject three fortuitously 'corrected' the version by his own 'mistake' and scored four marks. The corrected version persisted through to subject seven.

34

Figure 1:4
The changes occurring on items 11 and 12 illustrate assimilation by distortion

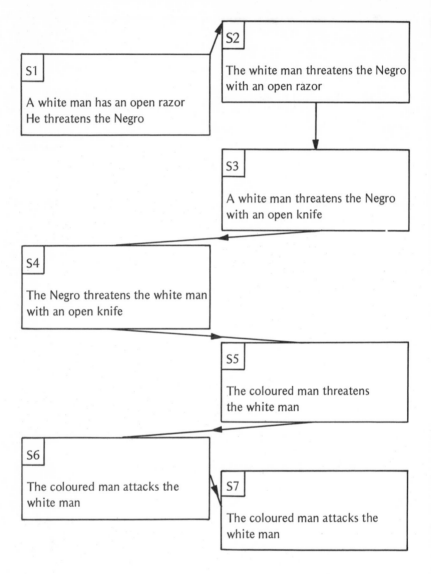

S1

A white man has an open razor
He threatens the Negro

S2

The white man threatens the Negro
with an open razor

S3

A white man threatens the Negro
with an open knife

S4

The Negro threatens the white man
with an open knife

S5

The coloured man threatens
the white man

S6

The coloured man attacks the
white man

S7

The coloured man attacks the
white man

Figure 1:5

(After Allport and Postman)

Table 1:5

Items					Subjects						Total
	1	2	3	4	5	6	7	8	9	10	score
1 The scene is a London railway station											
2 The station is Paddington											
3 Seven adults in the compartment											
4 Five are seated											
5 Two are standing											
6 Two are women											
7 One woman has a baby											
8 A Negro is standing											
9 He is well-dressed											
10 A white man is standing											
11 He threatens the Negro											
12 The white man has an open razor											
13 The women with the baby watches anxiously											
14 The other woman has a flowery hat											
15 She also has a fur collar on her coat											
16 A man is reading the *Daily Express*											
17 Another man is asleep											
18 There is a Jewish man											
19 He has a book on his knee											
20 There are advertisements for cigarettes, shoes, etc.											
Totals											

Scoring Instructions

1 Award two marks for a perfect or almost perfect reproduction of the original item as set down above.

2 Award one mark for a reasonably accurate reproduction which contains most of the sense of the item as set down on the checklist.

3 Award no marks for failure to mention the item at all.

4 In the space at the bottom of the checklist, make a short note of any interesting additions that subjects make when re-telling the story. To help identify the subject, put an S1, S2, S3 etc., after your note to identify the person.

Figure 1:6

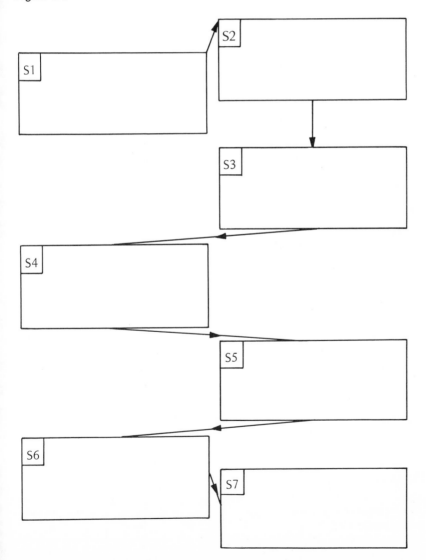

The audience is able to observe the changes that occur during the subjects' recitations by reference to the picture displayed throughout the experiment. The subjects use the tape-recording to observe the changes that occur.

Further applications

Read and discuss the following experiment:
LEVINE, J. M., and MURPHY, G. The Learning and Forgetting of Controversial Material, *Journal of Abnormal and Social Psychology*, 38, pp. 507–517, 1943.

What processes are reported in the above experiment that are similar to those you have found in conducting Experiment 3?

References

ALLPORT, G. W. and POSTMAN, L. J., The Basic Psychology of Rumour, in *MACCOBY, E. E., NEWCOMB, T. M., HARTLEY, E. L.*, (eds.), *Readings in Social Psychology*, Methuen, London, pp. 54–65, 1961.

STUDENTS' RATINGS OF DIFFERENT UNIVERSITIES

Aim:

To examine differences in the evaluations students make of different groups of universities.

University Rating Questionnaire

We would like you to rate certain groupings of universities below by means of a number of adjectival scales. On each scale we would like you to put a cross at the point which best expresses your rating. If, for example, you were asked to rate a certain group of universities on the scale good : : : : : : : bad and you thought that they were very good, then you would put a cross thus:

good : X : : : : : bad

If, on the other hand, you thought the group of universities to be very bad you would put a cross thus:

good : : : : : X : bad

If your judgments were less extreme you would use the intermediate points on the scale. Now go ahead to rate the following group of universities.

Civic universities (*e.g., Manchester, Leeds, Sheffield, Nottingham*)

Cultured	:___:___:___:___:___:___:	Uncultured
Conventional	:___:___:___:___:___:___:	Unconventional
Useful	:___:___:___:___:___:___:	Useless
Swinging	:___:___:___:___:___:___:	Dead
Undistinguished	:___:___:___:___:___:___:	Outstanding
Interesting	:___:___:___:___:___:___:	Uninteresting
Proud	:___:___:___:___:___:___:	Unpretentious
Free	:___:___:___:___:___:___:	Restricted
Dull	:___:___:___:___:___:___:	Exciting
Down to earth	:___:___:___:___:___:___:	Unworldly
Academically excellent	:___:___:___:___:___:___:	Academically poor

New emergent universities (*e.g., Lancaster, Kent, Sussex, Essex*)

Cultured	:___:___:___:___:___:___:	Uncultured
Conventional	:___:___:___:___:___:___:	Unconventional
Useful	:___:___:___:___:___:___:	Useless
Swinging	:___:___:___:___:___:___:	Dead
Undistinguished	:___:___:___:___:___:___:	Outstanding
Interesting	:___:___:___:___:___:___:	Uninteresting
Proud	:___:___:___:___:___:___:	Unpretentious
Free	:___:___:___:___:___:___:	Restricted
Dull	:___:___:___:___:___:___:	Exciting
Down to earth	:___:___:___:___:___:___:	Unworldly
Academically excellent	:___:___:___:___:___:___:	Academically poor

Oxbridge (*Oxford and Cambridge*)

Cultured	:___:___:___:___:___:___:	Uncultured
Conventional	:___:___:___:___:___:___:	Unconventional
Useful	:___:___:___:___:___:___:	Useless
Swinging	:___:___:___:___:___:___:	Dead
Undistinguished	:___:___:___:___:___:___:	Outstanding
Interesting	:___:___:___:___:___:___:	Uninteresting
Proud	:___:___:___:___:___:___:	Unpretentious
Free	:___:___:___:___:___:___:	Restricted
Dull	:___:___:___:___:___:___:	Exciting
Down to earth	:___:___:___:___:___:___:	Unworldly
Academically excellent	:___:___:___:___:___:___:	Academically poor

Ex-colleges of advanced technology (*e.g., Bradford, Bath, Salford, Loughborough*)

Cultured	:___:___:___:___:___:___:	Uncultured
Conventional	:___:___:___:___:___:___:	Unconventional
Useful	:___:___:___:___:___:___:	Useless
Swinging	:___:___:___:___:___:___:	Dead
Undistinguished	:___:___:___:___:___:___:	Outstanding
Interesting	:___:___:___:___:___:___:	Uninteresting
Proud	:___:___:___:___:___:___:	Unpretentious
Free	:___:___:___:___:___:___:	Restricted
Dull	:___:___:___:___:___:___:	Exciting
Down to earth	:___:___:___:___:___:___:	Unworldly
Academically excellent	:___:___:___:___:___:___:	Academically poor

Celtic universities (*e.g., Swansea, Cardiff, Aberystwyth*)

Cultured	:___:___:___:___:___:___:	Uncultured
Conventional	:___:___:___:___:___:___:	Unconventional
Useful	:___:___:___:___:___:___:	Useless
Swinging	:___:___:___:___:___:___:	Dead
Undistinguished	:___:___:___:___:___:___:	Outstanding
Interesting	:___:___:___:___:___:___:	Uninteresting
Proud	:___:___:___:___:___:___:	Unpretentious
Free	:___:___:___:___:___:___:	Restricted
Dull	:___:___:___:___:___:___:	Exciting
Down to earth	:___:___:___:___:___:___:	Unworldly
Academically excellent	:___:___:___:___:___:___:	Academically poor

Analysis

1   Separate male and female questionnaires.

2   For male and female groups on each of the 11 adjectival scales collate scores to obtain frequency distributions.

3   Differences between university groupings may be examined by chi-square within male and female groups separately at first before combining to examine differences between university groupings within the total sample.

Example

Cohen (1970) used semantic differential scales with some 507 sixth form boys and girls in four secondary schools in Northern England to examine differences in their perceptions of various university groups. Among other findings it was shown that boys were more favourable in their evaluations of ex-colleges of advanced technology such as Salford, Bradford and Loughborough than girls. In the total sample sixth formers saw Oxbridge as most cultured and the ex-colleges of advanced technology as least cultured. Conversely, whilst the new emergent universities such as Lancaster, Essex and Sussex were perceived as most free, Oxbridge was considered most restrictive.

In the same study, boys and girls were rated by their teachers according to their academic excellence. Two groups of sixth formers were identified — outstanding pupils, those likely to do exceptionally well in 'A'-levels, and border-line pupils, those likely to be pass/fail in 'A'-level examinations.

The following comparison of the perceptions of outstanding v. border-line pupils on the academic excellence of ex-colleges of advanced technology was reported.

CONCEPT: ex-colleges of advanced technology

Group	Academically excellent				Academically poor		Total
Outstanding pupils	0	5	22	18	9	2	56
Border-line pupils	9	21	31	8	1	0	70

Because of the small numbers in the 'academically excellent' and 'academically poor' cells the 2×6 distribution was collapsed to 2×3 and analysed by chi-square (see Appendix 2, Treatment 7, p. 205).

Outstanding pupils	5	40	11
Border-line pupils	30	39	1

$$\chi^2 = 24.95 \quad \text{d.f.} = 2 \quad p < 0.01$$

The difference in the ratings of the two groups of pupils is highly significant. Why should border-line pupils rate ex-colleges of advanced technology so much more highly on academic excellence than outstanding pupils?

_____

_____

_____

_____

_____

Analysis

1   Select two groups of universities to be compared e.g. new emergents and civic universities.

2   In male (or female) respondent groups, compare the frequency distributions on each of the adjectival pairs (combine cells where necessary).

New emergents v. Civics

Cultured_____ Uncultured

New emergents						
Civics						

$\chi^2 =$_____d.f. = $p =$

Conventional_____Unconventional

New emergents						
Civics						

$\chi^2 =$_____d.f. = $p =$

3   Continue for other groups of universities on other adjectival scales.

4   Compare male and female ratings of selected groups of universities on selected adjectival scales.

Further applications

1 Compute an 'A'-level score in Experiment 7 p. 74 for each respondent. Use this score to obtain an 'outstanding' and a 'border-line' group. Compare the evaluations of these two groups across selected adjectival scales and selected groups of universities. How do your results compare with those reported by Cohen (1970) in respect of sixth formers?

2 From the information given on the orange page devise a classification of respondents by subject area. Examine ratings of university groups by subject area.

3 Re-design p. 242 to obtain the following information:
First choice of university (or college)
Second choice of university (or college)
Third choice of university (or college)

Use the choice list to obtain evaluations of specific institutions. How do respondents' ratings of their first choices compare with their ratings of their actual institutions? Try to explain differences and the direction of those differences.

Reference

COHEN, L., Sixth Form Pupils and their Views of Higher Education. *Journal of Curriculum Studies*, **2**, 1, pp. 67–72, 1970.

PERCEIVING

The way in which we respond to the social environment is a function of our perceptions of the world about us. Each of us constructs a personal view of the world by responding at any one time to a minute part of the enormous amount of information continuously bombarding our sensory organs. We are selective in our perceptions because of the necessity of simplifying this vast array of sensory data before us and about us at any moment in time. We simplify in order to make sense of our environment, and making sense of our environment enables us to make it more predictable. It was Sir Frederick Bartlett who suggested that every cognitive reaction on our part might be seen as our effort after meaning.

In the Experiment 1 'conformity to norms' reference was made to the function of norms in providing shared rules by which we are able to order our social environment. By ordering the environment we make it more predictable; a shared ordering facilitates reciprocal behaviour with our fellow society members. Experiments 2 and 3 'social class stereotypes' and 'rumour' respectively, illustrated the function of perceptual processes such as distorting, levelling, sharpening and omitting in bringing to a complex mass of external stimuli a more simple structure to which we are better able to respond. Thus, 'catholics', 'coloureds' and 'communists' are broad classes of concepts to which we are able to react with relative ease. To respond to the unique attributes of each and every exemplar of these concepts would be quite impossible.

It should not be thought, however, that we passively await the impact of external stimuli before our selective perceptual processes begin to operate. The experiment which reported sixth formers' stereotypic views of various universities is an example of the dynamic aspect of perceiving. In Experiment 4 'students' ratings of different universities', it was shown that prior to any actual experience of university life, secondary schoolboys and schoolgirls had nevertheless developed distinctly stereotyped views of different groups of universities both in terms of their academic prowess and the quality of the social life on their respective campuses.

As well as demonstrating the function of perceptual processes in social interaction, Experiments 2 and 4 contained suggestions for further study which point to the special interest of the social psychologist in certain aspects of perceiving. In Experiment 2, the suggestion was made that subjects might be differentiated in terms of the openness or closedness of their belief systems prior to an exploration of their social class stereotyping. In Experiment 4, it was suggested that subjects might be identified as outstandingly able academically or less able academically before an examination of their ratings of universities. A particular interest of the social psychologist in the study of social perception is that of the effect of personal and social factors upon the processes of perceiving. How different, for example, are the social class stereotypes of highly dogmatic individuals in comparison with their less dogmatic fellow beings? How does high academic ability (and, presumably, greater 'chance' of university acceptance) affect the ways in which boys and girls perceive different universities? These are important and interesting questions which users of this text may wish to pursue.

References

ALLEN, V. L., Situational factors in Conformity. In L. Berkowitz (Ed.), *Advances in Experimental Social Psychology,* Academic Press, New York, Vol. 2, pp. 133–175, 1965.

BERG, I. A. and BASS, B. M., (Eds) Conformity and Deviation, Harper and Row, New York, 1961.

BYRNE, D. and WONG, T. J., Racial Prejudice, Interpersonal Attraction and Assumed Dissimilarity of Attitudes, *Journal of Abnormal and Social Psychology,* 65, pp. 246–253, 1962.

KELSALL, R. K., and KELSALL, H. M., The School Teacher in England and the United States, Pergamon Press, Oxford, pp. 67–81, 1969.

KRAMER, E., Judgment of Personal Characteristics and Emotions from Non-verbal Properties of Speech, *Psychological Bulletin,* 60, pp. 408–420, 1962.

National Opinion Poll, Nos 109, 110, June 1972.

SECORD, P. F. BEVAN, W. and DUKES, W. F., Occupational and Physiognomic Stereotypes in the Perception of Photographs, *Journal of Social Psychology,* 37, pp. 261–270, 1953.

TAJFEL, H., Social and Cultural Factors in Perception. In G. Lindzey, and E. Aronson, (Eds), *Handbook of Social Psychology,* Addison-Wesley, Reading, Mass., Vol. 3, pp. 315–394, 1969.

TAJFEL, H., Cognitive Aspects of Prejudice, *Journal of Biosocial Science Supplement,* 1, pp. 173–191, 1969.

VENESS, T. and BRIERLY, D. W., Forming Impressions of Personality: Two Experiments, *British Journal of Social and Clinical Psychology,* 2, pp. 11–19, 1963.

EXPECTATIONS IN DIFFERENT ORGANIZATIONS

Aim:

To examine the different types of power that govern superordinate—subordinate relationships in different organizations.

Method

A five-item questionnaire with accompanying instructions is administered to the subject group as a paper-and-pencil test.

Questionnaire

Below are listed five reasons often given by_____ (name the target group, e.g. student teachers, sandwich course students, etc.) when asked why they do what their _____ (name the target group, e.g. college tutors, industry-based supervisors, etc.) ask them to do. Please indicate how important each reason is to you for causing you to carry out your_____ s instructions by putting a tick in the appropriate 'box'.

		Very important	Quite important	Not very important	Not important at all
1	Because I respect his/her position of authority which gives him/her the right to make decisions about my work.	☐	☐	☐	☐
2	Because I know that he/she is constantly checking my work with a view to reporting on my performance to the_____ (name the appropriate body or individual, e.g. office manager, etc.)	☐	☐	☐	☐
3	Because I know he/she will quickly apply pressures to enforce his/her decisions if they are not carried out fully or properly.	☐	☐	☐	☐
4	Because I appreciate his/her greater ability and knowledge about aspects of the work which I have to do.	☐	☐	☐	☐
5	Because he/she is friendly and treats me more as an equal rather than someone who works under his/her direction.	☐	☐	☐	☐

Where the investigator collects data by individual interview the wording of the instructions and questionnaire items is altered as follows.

Here are five reasons often given by_____ (name the target group, e.g. shop-assistants, nursing cadets, apprentices, etc.) when asked why they do what their immediate supervisor asks them to do. Tell me how important each of the reasons is for causing you to carry out your supervisor's instructions.

	Very important	Quite important	Not very important	Not important at all
1 Because I respect his/her position of authority which gives him/her the right to make decisions about my work.	☐	☐	☐	☐
2 Because I know that he/she is constantly checking my work with a view to reporting on my performance to the _____ (name the appropriate body or individual, e.g. office manager, etc.)	☐	☐	☐	☐
3 Because I know he/she will quickly apply pressures to enforce his/her decisions if they are not carried out fully or properly.	☐	☐	☐	☐
4 Because I appreciate his/her greater ability and knowledge about aspects of the work I have to do.	☐	☐	☐	☐
5 Because he/she is friendly and treats me more as an equal rather than someone who works under his/her direction.	☐	☐	☐	☐

Analysis

Each of the five questionnaire statements is analysed separately by chi-square (see Appendix 2, Treatment 7, p. 205), or by a test for the significance of the difference between two observed proportions (see Appendix 2, Treatment 13, p. 216). Researchers should select the target population (e.g. student teachers on school practice, nursing cadets, sandwich course students, factory employees) and decide the most appropriate method of collecting the data on supervisor student relationships. A fairly large sample is desirable (50–80) if the necessity of combining adjacent cells in the response continuum is to be avoided. With smaller samples it might be considered desirable to use a response continuum consisting simply of:

Important   Not important

Chi-square analysis with Yates' Correction (see Appendix 2, Treatment 7, p. 205), would be an appropriate technique for analysis of data cast in this 2 x 2 form.

Example
By way of example, the responses of 78 university undergraduates on 6-month sandwich courses in industry (Cohen, 1971) are compared with those of 91 male student-teachers on their final school practice. Each type of power in supervisor/student relationships is analysed separately.

Legitimate Power   *supervisor's right to direct*

Target group	n	Very important	Quite important	Not very important	Not important at all
Sandwich students	78	11	40	22	5
Student teachers	91	2	19	47	23

$$\chi^2 = 33.52 \quad \text{d.f. } 3 \quad p < 0.01$$

Reward Power   *supervisor's evaluating and reporting*

Target group	n	Very important	Quite important	Not very important	Not important at all
Sandwich students	78	9	25	27	17
Student teachers	91	4	19	36	36

$$\chi^2 = 9.01 \quad \text{d.f. } 3 \quad p < 0.05$$

Coercive Power *supervisor's ability to punish*

Target group	n	Very important	Quite important	Not very important	Not important at all
Sandwich students	78	1	3	34	40
Student teachers	91	0	1	52	38

The distribution of responses in respect of coercive power (above) does not permit the use of chi-square as a means of analysis. It is possible, however, to determine whether or not a significantly greater proportion of sandwich course students than student teachers record the view that their supervisor's coercive power is 'not very important' or 'not important at all'. A test for the significance of the difference between two observed proportions is appropriate (Brown, 1956). A full account of the test is given in Appendix 2, Treatment 13, p. 216 of this book.

Expert Power *supervisor's knowledge and skills*

Target group	n	Very important	Quite important	Not very important	Not important at all
Sandwich students	78	33	34	7	4
Student teachers	91	35	35	12	9

$$\chi^2 = 2.32 \quad \text{d.f. 3} \quad p \text{ . ns}$$

Referent Power *supervisor's friendliness*

Target group	n	Very important	Quite important	Not very important	Not important at all
Sandwich students	78	30	34	7	7
Student teachers	91	18	24	23	16

$$\chi^2 = 16.72 \quad \text{d.f. 3} \quad p < 0.01$$

In summary, sandwich course students stressed more strongly than student teachers the importance of the supervisor's legitimate power (his right to direct them) his reward power (his evaluating and reporting on their work) and his referent power (his friendliness towards them). Neither group, apparently, experienced the use of coercive power by their respective supervisors and both groups of students referred to the supervisor's expert power (his knowledge and skills) as an important source of their motivation to comply with his directives.

Interpret the above differences in the reported use of power in the light of the following additional information about the respective organizational settings in which students were placed.

1 The sandwich course students were largely engaged in production-line work with regular quality-control checks.

2 The student teachers were on their final school practice during which time it is customary for the student to assume full responsibility for the classes he teaches.

_____

_____

_____

_____

_____

_____

Analysis

1 Classify responses of selected target groups using the tables below.
2 Employ chi-square to examine differences in the frequency distributions of the target groups.
3 When frequency distributions are highly skewed, use the Brown test for significance of differences between two proportions to compare selected cells.

Legitimate power   *supervisor's right to direct*

Target group	n	Very important	Quite important	Not very important	Not important at all

52

Reward Power   *supervisor's evaluating and reporting*

Target group	n	Very important	Quite important	Not very important	Not important at all

Coercive Power   *supervisor's ability to punish*

Target group	n	Very important	Quite important	Not very important	Not important at all

Expert Power   *supervisor's knowledge and skills*

Target group	n	Very important	Quite important	Not very important	Not important at all

Referent Power   *supervisor's friendliness*

Target group	n	Very important	Quite important	Not very important	Not important at all

Further applications

1   Examine the relationship between the type of power exercised by supervisors and the degree of satisfaction/dissatisfaction recorded by those they supervise. Use the following adaptation of a job-satisfaction scale originally designed by Start (1966) for use with teachers.

Please put a tick in the appropriate box to show how satisfied or dissatisfied you are with your relationship with your supervisor.

I am:

☐   Most dissatisfied

☐   Less satisfied than many of my colleagues (fellow students, mates, etc.)

☐   As satisfied as the majority of my colleagues (fellow students, mates, etc.)

☐   More satisfied than most of my colleagues (fellow students, mates, etc.)

☐   Very satisfied

☐   Extremely satisfied

2   During a school practice period explore the proposition that female student teachers supervised by male class teachers experience different types of power in the supervisor/student relationship from those experienced by male student teachers supervised by male class teachers.

References

BROWN, I., A Significance Test for the Difference Between Two Observed Proportions. *Occupational Psychology*, 30, pp. 169–174. 1956.

COHEN, L., Anxiety, Ambiguity and Supervisory Style in Relation to Students' Evaluation of Their thin Sandwich Course Experience. *Bulletin of Mechanical Engineering Education*, 10, pp. 297–302, 1971.

START, K. B., The Success of a Group of Teachers in Relation to Their Personal and Professional Background. Unpublished PhD thesis, University of Manchester, 1966.

ROLE CONFLICT

Aim

To examine role conflict in the setting of a college of education*.

Method

Role A   Write down two types of behaviour expected of a student who is determined to do exceptionally well in his academic course work.

1 _____

2 _____

Role B   Write down two types of behaviour necessary for popularity with other students.

1 _____

2 _____

Role C   Write down two types of behaviour expected by the supervising tutor on school practice.

1 _____

2 _____

Role D   Write down two types of behaviour expected by the classroom teacher on school practice.

1 _____

2 _____

Role E   Write down two types of behaviour parents might expect of their son or daughter as a student.

1 _____

2 _____

*Note:
This experiment may be used in a variety of other situations, see note on p. 68.

On the scales below, assume that:

     0   means the roles are *complementary*, i.e. they reinforce one another.

     5   means the roles have *no relationship* to each other.

    10   means the roles *conflict* one with another.

Assume that the two descriptions you have provided on the previous page form a single definition of that role.

    On each of the scales below circle the number that best shows how much the roles (as you have described them) reinforce or conflict with each other.

Roles A — B   Academic success — student popularity

Reinforces					Neutral				Conflicts	
0	1	2	3	4	5	6	7	8	9	10

Roles A — C   Academic success — supervising tutor

Reinforces					Neutral				Conflicts	
0	1	2	3	4	5	6	7	8	9	10

Roles A — D   Academic success — classroom teacher

Reinforces					Neutral				Conflicts	
0	1	2	3	4	5	6	7	8	9	10

Roles A — E   Academic success — parents' wishes

Reinforces					Neutral				Conflicts	
0	1	2	3	4	5	6	7	8	9	10

Roles B — C   Student popularity — supervising tutor

Reinforces					Neutral				Conflicts	
0	1	2	3	4	5	6	7	8	9	10

Roles B – D   Student popularity – classroom teacher

Reinforces					Neutral					Conflicts
0	1	2	3	4	5	6	7	8	9	10

Roles B – E   Student popularity – parents' wishes

Reinforces					Neutral					Conflicts
0	1	2	3	4	5	6	7	8	9	10

Roles C – D   Supervising tutor – classroom teacher

Reinforces					Neutral					Conflicts
0	1	2	3	4	5	6	7	8	9	10

Roles C – E   Supervising tutor – parents' wishes

Reinforces					Neutral					Conflicts
0	1	2	3	4	5	6	7	8	9	10

Roles D – E   Classroom teacher – parents' wishes

Reinforces					Neutral					Conflicts
0	1	2	3	4	5	6	7	8	9	10

Computations

Work out the median for each of the pairs of roles and enter in Table 1:6 below (see Appendix 2 p. 191).

Table 1:6

Paired roles	Median
AB	
AC	
AD	
AE	
BC	
BD	
BE	
CD	
CE	
DE	

Beginning with the most conflicting pair of roles, i.e. the one with the highest median, place the paired roles in rank order Table 1:7 below ranging from the most to the least conflicting.

Table 1:7

Rank order	Paired roles	Median
1		
2		
3		
4		
5		
6		
7		
8		
9		
10		

Analysis

In a study of role conflict in a college of education setting, student teachers were randomly selected from each of the three year groups, 17 first-year, 17 second-year and 18 third-year students. Table 1:8 below shows medians of each of the three-year groups (taken individually) and the rank ordering of those medians.

Table 1:8

Median conflict scores of three student-teacher groups
Sample — 52 female college students.

Year 1			Year 2			Year 3		
Role	Median	Rank order	Role	Median	Rank order	Role	Median	Rank order
AB	8.47	1	AB	7.72	1	AB	8.33	1
AC	3.35	10	AC	4.11	8	AC	3.73	9
AD	4.23	7	AD	4.55	5	AD	4.33	7
AE	3.82	9	AE	4.39	6	AE	3.00	10
BC	5.88	3	BC	3.83	9	BC	6.33	4
BD	5.17	4	BD	4.27	7	BD	6.73	3
BE	6.88	2	BE	4.77	2	BE	7.26	2
CD	3.94	8	CD	3.39	10	CD	3.86	8
CE	4.82	5	CE	4.58	4	CE·	4.46	5
DE	4.29	6	DE	4.61	3	DE	4.40	6

Inspection of Table 1:8 shows roles A to B to be the most conflicting for each of the three student groups, all three assigning it rank order 1. Similarly, Roles B to E are unanimously assigned second place in order of conflict. There appears to be a fair measure of agreement among the three groups in respect of their rank ordering. If we wish to know more accurately, however, whether or not significant differences occur between the three student groups in their perceptions of role conflict we must use an appropriate statistical analysis.

The Kruskal—Wallis one-way analysis of variance by ranks (see Appendix 2, Treatment 6, p. 202) enables us to decide whether or not significant differences in the rankings of role conflict occur between student years.

In Table 1:9 below the median conflict scores of *all three* student groups are simultaneously ranked from lowest to highest. These ranks are then summed to obtain $R_1 = 159$, $R_2 = 145$ and $R_3 = 161$.

Table 1:9
Rank ordering of role conflict scores of three student-teacher groups

Year 1			Year 2			Year 3		
Role	Median	Rank order	Role	Median	Rank order	Role	Median	Rank order
AB	8.47	30	AB	7.72	28	AB	8.33	29
AC	3.35	2	AC	4.11	9	AC	3.73	4
AD	4.23	10	AD	4.55	17	AD	4.33	13
AE	3.82	5	AE	4.39	14	AE	3.00	1
BC	5.88	23	BC	3.83	6	BC	6.33	24
BD	5.17	22	BD	4.27	11	BD	6.73	25
BE	6.88	26	BE	4.77	20	BE	7.26	27
CD	3.94	8	CD	3.39	3	CD	3.86	7
CE	4.82	21	CE	4.58	18	CE	4.46	16
DE	4.29	12	DE	4.61	19	DE	4.40	15
	$R_1 = 159$			$R_2 = 145$			$R_3 = 161$	

Analysis of these data by the Kruskal–Wallis test gives a value of $H = 0.19$ with 2 d.f. A value of 5.99 is required for H to be significant at the 0.05 level. Clearly, the value obtained indicates that with respect to their role conflict scores our three student-teacher groups must be assumed to have been drawn from the same population. That is, there are no significant differences between them.

Suppose that in the present experiment we had collected role conflict data in Years 1 and 2 only, or that we wished to examine the degree of relationship between the rankings in Years 1 and 2 only, Spearman's rank order correlation coefficient (r_s), is an appropriate statistic by which to obtain a measure of that association (see Appendix 2, Treatment 8, p. 208).

Table 1:10
Rank orderings in role conflict:
Year 1 and Year 2 compared by Spearman's r_s

Rank ordering by Year 1		Rank ordering by Year 2			
Roles	Rank order	Roles	Rank order	d	d^2
AB	1	AB	1	0	0
BE	2	BE	2	0	0
BC	3	BC	9	6	36
BD	4	BD	7	3	9
CE	5	CE	4	1	1
DE	6	DE	3	3	9
AD	7	AD	5	2	4
CD	8	CD	10	2	4
AE	9	AE	6	3	9
AC	10	AC	8	2	4
					d^2 76

$$r_s = 1 - \frac{6 \times 76}{10(10-1)(10+1)}$$

$$r_s = 1 - \frac{456}{990}$$

$$r_s = 0.539$$

With large samples where n is 10 or more the significance of r_s may be tested by the t test (see Appendix 2, Treatment 9, p. 210). For d.f. = 8 a t value of 2.306 must be obtained for significance at the 0.05 level. Our value (1.804) falls short of that figure. We conclude that the role conflict rank orderings of Years 1 and 2 are not significantly associated.

Role A Write down two types of behaviour expected of a student who is determined to do exceptionally well in his academic course work.

1_____

2_____

Role B Write down two types of behaviour necessary for popularity with other students.

1_____

2_____

Role C Write down two types of behaviour expected by the supervising tutor on school practice.

1_____

2_____

Role D Write down two types of behaviour expected by the classroom teacher on school practice.

1_____

2_____

Role E Write down two types of behaviour parents might expect of their son or daughter as a student.

1_____

2_____

On the scales below, assume that:

    0   means the roles are complementary, i.e. they reinforce one another.

    5   means the roles have no relationship to each other.

    10 means the roles conflict one with another.

Assume that the two descriptions you have provided on the previous page form a single definition of that role.

    On each of the scales below circle the number that best shows how much the roles (as you have described them) reinforce or conflict with each other.

Roles A — B   Academic success — student popularity
___

Reinforces   Neutral   Conflicts

  0   1   2   3   4   5   6   7   8   9   10

Roles A — C   Academic success — supervising tutor
___

Reinforces   Neutral   Conflicts

  0   1   2   3   4   5   6   7   8   9   10

Roles A — D   Academic success — classroom teacher
___

Reinforces   Neutral   Conflicts

  0   1   2   3   4   5   6   7   8   9   10

Roles A — E   Academic success — parents' wishes
___

Reinforces   Neutral   Conflicts

  0   1   2   3   4   5   6   7   8   9   10

Roles B — C   Student popularity — supervising tutor
___

Reinforces   Neutral   Conflicts

  0   1   2   3   4   5   6   7   8   9   10

Roles B — D   Student popularity — classroom teacher

Reinforces				Neutral					Conflicts	
0	1	2	3	4	5	6	7	8	9	10

Roles B — E   Student popularity — parents' wishes

Reinforces				Neutral					Conflicts	
0	1	2	3	4	5	6	7	8	9	10

Roles C — D   Supervising tutor-classroom teacher

Reinforces				Neutral					Conflicts	
0	1	2	3	4	5	6	7	8	9	10

Roles C — E   Supervising tutor — parents' wishes

Reinforces				Neutral					Conflicts	
0	1	2	3	4	5	6	7	8	9	10

Roles D — E   Classroom teacher — parents' wishes

Reinforces				Neutral					Conflicts	
0	1	2	3	4	5	6	7	8	9	10

Computations

Work out the median for each of the pairs of roles and enter in Table 1:11 below (see Appendix 2, Treatment 2, p. 191).

Table 1:11

Paired roles	Median
AB	
AC	
AD	
AE	
BC	
BD	
BE	
CD	
CE	
DE	

Beginning with the most conflicting pair of roles, i.e. the one with the highest median, place the paired roles in rank order in Table 1:12 below, ranging from the most to the least conflicting.

Table 1:12

Rank order	Paired roles	Median
1		
2		
3		
4		
5		
6		
7		
8		
9		
10		

Table 1:13
Median Conflict Scores

Group 1			Group 2			Group 3		
Role	Median	Rank	Role	Median	Rank	Role	Median	Rank
AB			AB			AB		
AC			AC			AC		
AD			AD			AD		
AE			AE			AE		
BC			BC			BC		
BD			BD			BD		
BE			BE			BE		
CD			CD			CD		
CE			CE			CE		
DE			DE			DE		
	$R_1 =$			$R_2 =$			$R_3 =$	

$$H = \frac{12}{N(N+1)} \frac{R_j^2}{n_j} - 3(N+1)$$

$$H = \frac{12}{\underline{\hspace{1cm}}} \left[\frac{}{\underline{\hspace{2cm}}} + \frac{}{\underline{\hspace{2cm}}} + \frac{}{\underline{\hspace{2cm}}} \right] - 3(\quad)$$

$$=$$

$$= \underline{\hspace{2cm}} \quad \text{d.f.} = \underline{\hspace{2cm}} \quad p = \underline{\hspace{2cm}}$$

Interpret your findings briefly below.

_____

_____

_____

_____

Table 1:14
Comparing rank ordering in two groups

Rank ordering by Group 1		Rank ordering by Group 2		d	d^2
Roles	Order	Roles	Order		

d^2

$$r_s = 1 - \frac{6\Sigma(d)^2}{n(n-1)(n+1)}$$

$$r_s = 1 - \rule{3cm}{0.4pt}$$

$$= \rule{4cm}{0.4pt}$$

Testing the significance of r_s for small samples

Using Table A2:8 (p. 220) in Appendix 2, interpolate at the appropriate n and read across to obtain the r_s value at the 0.05 and the 0.01 levels of statistical significance. Interpret your findings briefly below.

_____

_____

_____

_____

For larger samples (by t test)

$$t = \sqrt{r_s \frac{n-2}{1-r_s^2}}$$

$t =$ _____

$=$ _____

$\text{d.f.} = n - 2 =$

Using Table 2.10 p. 228.
Interpolate at the appropriate degrees of freedom column to obtain the t value at 0.05 or 0.01 levels of significance. Interpret your findings briefly below.

_____

_____

_____

_____

Suggestions for further work

Designing a role conflict study

1   Interview a representative sample of the target population to find out which roles are generally seen to be conflicting in some way. One indirect way to obtain such information is to encourage interviewees to talk about their worries or problems. A more structured way is to use problem checklists. (see Cohen 1972(a), 1972(b)).

2   Design your written instructions to your role questionnaire (see page 54) in the light of item 1 above.

3   Within universities, polytechnics, and colleges of education, *sex, age, subject areas*, all suggest bases for grouping students to explore the intensity and direction of conflicting roles.

Lest the reader should assume that interviewing is merely a matter of asking *x* number of people *y* number of questions, Kerlinger's (1969) observation is appropriate at this juncture: 'Interviewing itself is an art, but the planning and writing of an interview schedule is even more of an art.' The reader is referred to relevant chapters in the following texts before embarking upon any interview work:

Payne, S. L., *The Art of Asking Questions*, Princeton University Press, 1951.

Festinger, L. and Katz, D., (Eds.) *Research Methods in the Behavioral Sciences*, Holt, Rinehart and Winston, New York, Chap. 8, 1953.

Parten, M., *Surveys, Polls, and Samples*, Harper and Row, New York, Chap. 6, 1950.

References

COHEN, L., School to College: Some Initial Problems of Adjustment Among First Year Student Teachers, *Education for Development*, 2, 2, pp. 3–9, 1972(a).

COHEN, L., Personality and Problems in a College of Education Environment, *Durham Research Review*, 6, 28, pp. 617–622, 1972(b).

DEAN, D. G. and VALDES, D. M., *Experiments in Sociology*, Appleton—Century—Crofts, New York, 1963.

KELVIN, P., *The Bases of Social Behaviour*, Holt, Rinehart and Winston, Ltd, London, Chap. 5, 1969.

KERLINGER, F. N., *Foundations of Behavioral Research*, Holt, Rinehart and Winston, London, 1969.

SELF-IDENTITIES AND BEHAVIOUR IN ORGANIZATIONS

Aim

To identify student self-identities and the different behaviours that are associated with them.

Method

Prior to the adminstration to the self-identity questionnaire students have been asked to complete a number of requests for information about themselves. It should be stressed again at this point that nowhere should the student write his name or anything that may in any way identify him. The clear guarantee of *absolute anonymity* is important to the success of the exercise.

Self-Identity Questionnaires

Sixteen-item self-identity questionnaires developed through factor analytical techniques by Cohen and Toomey (1973) for use with university students and by Mannion (1974) for use with college of education students are set out below with instructions for their completion.

University form

As a student, how much are you like the following kinds of persons? Please reply by circling one of the numbers on each of the scales below. A circle round a number at or near 9 shows you are very much like the person described. A circle round a number at or near 1 shows you are not at all like the person described. Intermediate values show differing degrees of likeness.

		Very much like me Not at all like me
Item		9 8 7 6 5 4 3 2 1
1	A person who takes part in university life outside the classroom.	9 8 7 6 5 4 3 2 1
2	A person who is very interested in his chosen subject.	9 8 7 6 5 4 3 2 1
3	A good mixer who gets on well with other students.	9 8 7 6 5 4 3 2 1
4	A person whose social life during term is largely within the university.	9 8 7 6 5 4 3 2 1
5	A person who enjoys the intellectual life of the university.	9 8 7 6 5 4 3 2 1
6	A person with the capacity to tackle his work and examinations successfully.	9 8 7 6 5 4 3 2 1
7	A person who enjoys the freedom of student life.	9 8 7 6 5 4 3 2 1
8	A person who cares more for fundamental values than for merely getting a degree.	9 8 7 6 5 4 3 2 1
9	A person who is popular with the opposite sex.	9 8 7 6 5 4 3 2 1
10	A person who sees his university studies primarily as a means to a successful career.	9 8 7 6 5 4 3 2 1
11	A person who spends a lot of time in solitary study.	9 8 7 6 5 4 3 2 1
12	A person who came to university to have a good time.	9 8 7 6 5 4 3 2 1
13	A person whose main concern is to obtain a qualification.	9 8 7 6 5 4 3 2 1
14	A person who spends considerable time thinking about and discussing social and/or political reform.	9 8 7 6 5 4 3 2 1
15	A person who believes that working on his own is more valuable than attending lectures.	9 8 7 6 5 4 3 2 1
16	A person who spends a lot of time outside class in social contact with fellow students.	9 8 7 6 5 4 3 2 1

College form

As a student, how much are you like the following kinds of persons? Please reply by circling one of the numbers on each of the scales below. A circle round a number at or near 9 shows you are very much like the person described. A circle round a number at or near 1 shows you are not at all like the person described. Intermediate values show differing degrees of likeness.

		Very much like me							Not at all like me

Item 9 8 7 6 5 4 3 2 1

Item		
1	A person who takes part in college life outside the classroom.	9 8 7 6 5 4 3 2 1
2	A person who is interested in his chosen subjects.	9 8 7 6 5 4 3 2 1
3	A good mixer who gets on well with other students.	9 8 7 6 5 4 3 2 1
4	A person whose social life during term is largely within or centred around the college.	9 8 7 6 5 4 3 2 1
5	A person who enjoys the intellectual life of the college.	9 8 7 6 5 4 3 2 1
6	A person with the capacity to tackle his work and examinations successfully.	9 8 7 6 5 4 3 2 1
7	A person who enjoys the freedom of student life.	9 8 7 6 5 4 3 2 1
8	A person who cares more for fundamental values than for merely getting a teaching qualification.	9 8 7 6 5 4 3 2 1
9	A person who is popular with the opposite sex.	9 8 7 6 5 4 3 2 1
10	A person who sees his college studies primarily as a means to a successful career.	9 8 7 6 5 4 3 2 1
11	A person who spends a lot of time in solitary study.	9 8 7 6 5 4 3 2 1
12	A person who came to college to have a good time.	9 8 7 6 5 4 3 2 1
13	A person whose main concern is to obtain a qualification.	9 8 7 6 5 4 3 2 1
14	A person who spends considerable time thinking about and discussing social and/or political reform.	9 8 7 6 5 4 3 2 1
15	A person who believes that working on his own is more valuable than attending lectures.	9 8 7 6 5 4 3 2 1
16	A person who spends a lot of time outside class in social contact with fellow students.	9 8 7 6 5 4 3 2 1

Scoring the Self-Identity Questionnaire

Analyses in both universities and colleges of education have shown that various items on the self-identity questionnaire 'cluster' together suggesting certain identifiable student self-identity groups (see Cohen and Toomey 1973). These have been named as follows:

The University Self-Identity Questionnaire

Items* 1, 4, 5, 3 and 16 indicate the *social intellectual* self-identity, referring to the student who takes part in university life outside the classroom, whose social life is largely within the university, who enjoys the intellectual life of the university and is a good mixer, spending a lot of time outside lectures in social contact with his fellow students. Score *social intellectual* self-identity by adding up the scores that the student obtains on each of the five items identified above.

Items* 12, 16, 9, 11(−) and 15 indicate the *social fun* self-identity, describing the student who comes up to university primarily to have a good time, spending much of his out-of-class time in social activities with fellow students. He sees himself as popular with the opposite sex, not given to spending a lot of time in solitary study, a good mixer who enjoys the freedom that accompanies university life. Score *social fun* self-identity by adding up the scores that the student obtains on each of the four positive items and subtracting the score that he obtains on item 11 above.

Items* 13, 10 and 8(−) indicate the *vocational* self-identity, describing the student whose primary concern in coming up to university is to obtain a qualification and who sees his university studies as preparation for a successful career. The vocationalist cares more for getting his degree than for fundamental values. Score *vocational* self-identity by adding up the scores that the student obtains on the two positive items and subtracting the score that he obtains on item 8 above.

Items* 15, 14 and 8 indicate the *reformer* self-identity, describing the student who spends a considerable amount of his time thinking about and discussing social reform and fundamental values. The reformer, moreover, believes that working on his own is probably more advantageous than attending lectures. Score *reformer* self-identity by adding up the scores that the student obtains on the three positive items identified above.

Items* 6, 2 and 11 indicate the *academic* self-identity, describing the student who has the capacity to tackle both work and examinations successfully and who demonstrates his great interest in his chosen subject by his industrious pursuit of solitary study.

*The order in which the items are given is indicative of the strength or the contribution of the first one or two items in defining the specific student self-identity.

The College of Education Self-Identity Questionnaire

Items 16, 4, 1, 12, 9 and 3 indicate the *social-fun* self-identity among college students. Score *social fun* self-identity by adding up the scores that the student obtains on each of the six items identified above.

Items 6, 5, 2, 11 and 3 indicate the *academic-intellectual* self-identity, among college students. Score *academic-intellectual* self-identity by adding up the scores that the student obtains on each of the five items identified above.

Items 13, 10 and 8(−) indicate the *vocational* self-identity among college students. Score *vocational* self-identity by adding up the scores that the student obtains on the two positive items and subtracting the score that he obtains on item 8 above.

Items 15, 14 and 8 indicate the *reformer* self-identity among college students. Score *reformer* self-identity by adding up the scores that the student obtains on the three positive items indentified above.

Computations

1   For each student calculate his/her score on each of the four or five self-identity 'clusters' and enter it as in Table 1:15. By way of example the university form together with its five clusters of items has been used below. College of education students' scores would be entered on a college form with its four clusters of items.

Table 1:15

	SELF-IDENTITY SCORES				
Student	Social intellectual	Social fun	Vocational	Reformer	Academic
1					
2					
3					
4					
5					
6					
7					
8					
9					
.					
.					
.					
n					
	$\bar{x} =$	$\bar{x} =$	$\bar{x} =$	$\bar{x} =$	$\bar{x} =$
	s.d. =	s.d. =	s.d. =	s.d. =	s.d. =

2   Calculate for each self-identity the mean score and s.d. (see Appendix 2, Treatments 1 and 3, pp. 190 and 194).

3   Using the mean score for each self-identity cluster, classify each student as 'high' (above the mean) and 'low' (below the mean) on each self-identity

grouping. Enter 'H' for high or 'L' for low in the spaces provided at the bottom of the orange introductory sheet. Hypothetical examples are given below.

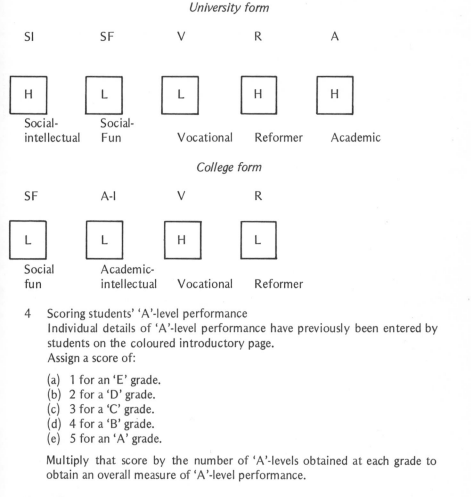

University form

SI	SF	V	R	A
H	L	L	H	H
Social-intellectual	Social-Fun	Vocational	Reformer	Academic

College form

SF	A-I	V	R
L	L	H	L
Social fun	Academic-intellectual	Vocational	Reformer

4   Scoring students' 'A'-level performance
Individual details of 'A'-level performance have previously been entered by students on the coloured introductory page.
Assign a score of:

(a) 1 for an 'E' grade.
(b) 2 for a 'D' grade.
(c) 3 for a 'C' grade.
(d) 4 for a 'B' grade.
(e) 5 for an 'A' grade.

Multiply that score by the number of 'A'-levels obtained at each grade to obtain an overall measure of 'A'-level performance.

Example:

E	D	C	B	A	
1	1	1			= Score 6

E	D	C	B	A	
	1		2	1	= Score 15

Analyses

It is now possible to test a variety of propositions about the association between specific student self-identities and students' abilities, residential accommodation, social relationships, and experience of 'clash' between academic and social activities. By way of example some data derived from a group of university students (Cohen and Toomey, 1973) are analysed to demonstrate a method of exploring the proposed associations. Some further hypotheses are then suggested about possible relationships between student self-identities and student behaviours which users may wish to test for themselves with their own data.

One hundred and twenty eight male undergraduates in Schools within the Board of Social Sciences at 'X' University were classified as 'high' or 'low' *academics* on the self-identity questionnaire. Table 1:16 below reports associations between academic self-identity and sections of the biographical data obtained on the orange introductory page.

Table 1:16
Academic Self-Identity and 'A'-Level Performance

Academic self-identity	n	'A'-level Performance		t test	p
		$\overline{x}$	s.d		
High	63	11.31	2.40		
Low	65	8.76	3.42	4.89	0.01

The appropriate statistical technique for the analysis above is a t test (see Appendix 2, Treatment 4, p. 196). The interpretation of Table 1:16 is that those social science students low on their academic self-identities came up to university with significantly poorer 'A'-levels than those high on their academic self-identities.

Table 1:17
Social Fun Self-Identity and 'Clash'

| Social fun self-identity | n | Degree of 'clash' | | | | | |
		None at all	Some	A fair amount	A considerable amount	A great degree	An enormous degree
High	64	2	5	13	28	14	2
Low	64	6	12	29	15	2	0

$$\chi^2 = 25.75 \quad \text{d.f. 3} \quad p < 0.01 \cdot$$

In the chi-square analysis above (Table 1:17), the 'none-at-all' and the 'some' categories have been collapsed into one category because of the requirement of at least 5 in the expected frequency distribution in any cell (see Appendix 2, Treatment 7, p. 205 for a note on this point). Similarly, it is necessary to collapse the 'enormous degree' category and the 'great degree' category into one composite score. Nevertheless the much greater degree of reported 'clash' between work and play in the high social-fun group is highly significant and in the direction that one would have predicted.

Other examples of analyses of the data on social science undergraduates concerned the relationships between their social-fun self-identities and their pattern of residential accommodation, and the proportion of the people with whom they spent their leisure activities who were also fellow students. An appropriate statistical technique for analysis in each of these cases is chi-square (see Appendix 2, Treatment 7, p. 205).

Table 1:18
Social Fun Self-Identity and Proportion of People in Social Activities who are Fellow Students

| Social fun Self-identity | n | Proportion of people who are fellow students | | | | | |
		None	Some	Fair number	Considerable number	Great number	All
High	64	1	4	8	12	23	16
Low	64	6	7	17	19	12	3

$$\chi^2 = 20.72 \quad \text{d.f. } 4 \quad p < 0.01$$

The chi-square value indicates that the high social fun self-identifiers spend their social activities in groups largely composed of fellow students to a significantly greater degree than low social fun self-identifiers. An interesting question which cannot unfortunately be answered from the present data concerns the extent to which continuing membership of such closely-interacting student groups helps to maintain and strengthen self-identities among their participants (see Cohen and Toomey 1973).

Table 1:19
Social Fun Self-Identity and Pattern of Residence

Social-fun Self-identity	n	Home	Alone in digs	Digs with other students	Hall of residence
High	64	6	7	10	41
Low	64	24	13	2	25

$$\chi^2 = 21.81 \quad \text{d.f. } 3 \quad p < 0.01$$

A high social fun self-identity appears to be associated with residence in a university hall rather than at home. The 'hall of residence' and the 'home' cells largely contribute to the difference between the two student groups.

Self-Identity Questionnaire

University form

As a student, how much are you like the following kinds of person? Please reply by circling one of the numbers on each of the scales below. A circle round a number at or near 9 shows you are very much like the person described. A circle round a number at or near 1 shows you are not at all like the person described. Intermediate values show differing degrees of likeness.

		Very much like me	Not at all like me
Item		9 8 7 6 5 4 3 2 1	
1	A person who takes part in university life outside the classroom.	9 8 7 6 5 4 3 2 1	
2	A person who is very interested in his chosen subject.	9 8 7 6 5 4 3 2 1	
3	A good mixer who gets on well with other students.	9 8 7 6 5 4 3 2 1	
4	A person whose social life during term is largely within the univesrity.	9 8 7 6 5 4 3 2 1	
5	A person who enjoys the intellectual life of the university.	9 8 7 6 5 4 3 2 1	
6	A person with the capacity to tackle his work and examinations successfully.	9 8 7 6 5 4 3 2 1	
7	A person who enjoys the freedom of student life.	9 8 7 6 5 4 3 2 1	
8	A person who cares more for fundamental values than for merely getting a degree.	9 8 7 6 5 4 3 2 1	
9	A person who is popular with the opposite sex.	9 8 7 6 5 4 3 2 1	
10	A person who sees his university studies primarily as a means to a successful career.	9 8 7 6 5 4 3 2 1	
11	A person who spends a lot of time in solitary study.	9 8 7 6 5 4 3 2 1	
12	A person who came to university to have a good time.	9 8 7 6 5 4 3 2 1	
13	A person whose main concern is to obtain a qualification.	9 8 7 6 5 4 3 2 1	
14	A person who spends considerable time thinking about and discussing social and/or political reform.	9 8 7 6 5 4 3 2 1	
15	A person who believes that working on his own is more valuable than attending lectures.	9 8 7 6 5 4 3 2 1	
16	A person who spends a lot of time outside class in social contact with fellow students.	9 8 7 6 5 4 3 2 1	

College form

As a student, how much are you like the following kinds of person? Please reply by circling one of the numbers on each of the scales below. A circle round a number at or near 9 shows you are very much like the person described. A circle round a number at or near 1 shows you are not at all like the person described. Intermediate values show differing degrees of likeness.

	Very much like me							Not at all like me

m   9 8 7 6 5 4 3 2 1

A person who takes part in college life
outside the classroom.   9 8 7 6 5 4 3 2 1

A person who is interested in his chosen
subjects.   9 8 7 6 5 4 3 2 1

A good mixer who gets on well with other
students.   9 8 7 6 5 4 3 2 1

A person whose social life during term is
largely within or centred around the college.   9 8 7 6 5 4 3 2 1

A person who enjoys the intellectual life of
the college.   9 8 7 6 5 4 3 2 1

A person with the capacity to tackle his work
and examinations successfully.   9 8 7 6 5 4 3 2 1

A person who enjoys the freedom of student
life.   9 8 7 6 5 4 3 2 1

A person who cares more for fundamental
values than for merely getting a teaching
qualification.   9 8 7 6 5 4 3 2 1

A person who is popular with the opposite
sex.   9 8 7 6 5 4 3 2 1

A person who sees his college studies
primarily as a means to a successful career.   9 8 7 6 5 4 3 2 1

A person who spends a lot of time in
solitary study.   9 8 7 6 5 4 3 2 1

A person who came to college to have a
good time.   9 8 7 6 5 4 3 2 1

A person whose main concern is to obtain
a qualification.   9 8 7 6 5 4 3 2 1

A person who spends considerable time
thinking about and discussing social and/or
political reform.   9 8 7 6 5 4 3 2 1

A person who believes that working on his
own is more valuable than attending lectures.   9 8 7 6 5 4 3 2 1

A person who spends a lot of time outside
class in social contact with fellow students.   9 8 7 6 5 4 3 2 1

Table 1:20

Follow instructions on p. 72 for scoring self-identity questionnaire. Enter each student's score in each column below.

SELF-IDENTITY SCORES (University form)

Student	Social-intellectual	Social-fun	Vocational	Reformer	Academic
1					
2					
3					
4					
5					
6					
7					
8					
9					
10					
11					
12					
13					
14					
15					
16					
17					
18					
19					
20					
21					
22					
23					
24					
25					
26					
27					
28					
29					
30					

(Reproduce this page and paste on if numbers require it.)

Table 1:21

Follow instructions on p. 73 for scoring self-identity questionnaire. Enter each student's score in each column below.

SELF-IDENTITY SCORES (College form)

Student	Social-fun	Academic- intellectual	Vocational	Reformer

(Reproduce this page and paste on if numbers require it.)

1 Calculate mean scores and standard deviations for the total student sample and enter in appropriate boxes below:

University form

Social-intellectual	
Mean	
s.d.	

Social-fun	
Mean	
s.d.	

Vocational	
Mean	
s.d.	

Reformer	
Mean	
s.d.	

Academic	
Mean	
s.d.	

College form

Social-fun	
Mean	
s.d.	

Academic-intellectual	
Mean	
s.d.	

Vocational	
Mean	
s.d.	

Reformer	
Mean	
s.d.	

2 Take, for example, the academic self-identity, classify each student as 'high' (above the mean) and 'low' (below the mean), and enter 'H' or 'L' in the appropriate box on the coloured page.

3 On the coloured page calculate each student's total 'A'-level score. (For instructions for scoring, see p. 75.)

4 Separate students' questionnaires into 'high' academic group and 'low' academic group.

5 Calculate the mean and standard deviation for the total 'A'-level scores of the 'high' academic group and the 'low' academic group.

6   Enter the data in the table below.

Table 1:22 Academic self-identity and 'A'-level performance

		'A'-level score			
Academic Self-Identity	n	$\bar{x}$	s.d.	t test	p
High					
Low					

    (H) High $\bar{x}$ =   (L) Low $\bar{x}$ =

    (H) High s.d. =   (L) Low s.d. =

    (H) High n =   (L) Low n =

$$t = \frac{\text{High } \bar{x} - \text{Low } \bar{x}}{\sqrt{\dfrac{\text{H s.d.}^2}{\text{H}n} + \dfrac{\text{L s.d.}^2}{\text{L}n}}}$$

$$t = \frac{-}{\sqrt{\rule{2cm}{0.4pt} + \rule{2cm}{0.4pt}}}$$

$$t = \frac{-}{\sqrt{\rule{2cm}{0.4pt} + \rule{2cm}{0.4pt}}} = \rule{3cm}{0.4pt} =$$

7   Interpret your findings in the above analysis and write them down briefly
below.

_____

_____

_____

_____

_____

_____

_____

8 Use the same procedures (classifying students as high or low on self-identities and collating biographical data from the coloured pages) to analyse the following:

Social-fun Self-identity	Degree of 'clash'					
	None at all	Some	A fair amount	A con-siderable amount	A great degree	An enor-mous degree
High						
Low						

	O						Total
High							
Low							

(Combine adjacent cells if necessary)

	E						Total
High							
Low							

	O–E						Total
High							
Low							

	$\dfrac{(O-E)^2}{E}$						Total
High							
Low							

$$\chi^2 = \Sigma \frac{(O-E)^2}{E} = \underline{\hspace{4cm}}$$

d.f. $= (r-1)(c-1) = \underline{\hspace{4cm}}$

Significance of chi-square $= \underline{\hspace{5cm}}$

9 Interpret your findings in the above analysis and write them down briefly below.

_____

_____

_____

_____

_____

10

Vocational self-identity	Hours per week spent in study					
	0–3	4–7	8–11	12–15	16–19	20 or more
High						
Low						

	O					Total
High						
Low						

(Combine adjacent cells if necessary)

	E					Total
High						
Low						

	$O–E$					Total
High						
Low						

	$\dfrac{(O–E)^2}{E}$					Total
High						
Low						

$$\chi^2 = \Sigma \frac{(O-E)^2}{E} = \underline{\hspace{4cm}}$$

d.f. = $(r-1)(c-1)$ = \underline{\hspace{3cm}}

Significance of chi-square = \underline{\hspace{3cm}}

11 Interpret your findings in the above analysis and write them down briefly below.

\underline{\hspace{12cm}}

\underline{\hspace{12cm}}

\underline{\hspace{12cm}}

\underline{\hspace{12cm}}

\underline{\hspace{12cm}}

\underline{\hspace{12cm}}

Further applications

Re-design the biographical data request on the coloured back page to obtain information on students' main subject(s), their involvement in Student Union activities and their predictions of the likely quality of their final degree award (or equivalent).

Develop a profile of the reformer self-identity. Examine the hypothesis that the reformer is likely to be male, from the social sciences, above average in 'A'-level performance, and expecting to do well in final awards.

References

COHEN, L. and TOOMEY, D., Role Orientations and Subcultures Among Undergraduate Students — An Empirical Investigation in a Technological University, Research in Education (in press), 1973.

FELDMAN, K. A., Studying the Impacts of Colleges on Students, Sociology of Education, 42, 3, pp. 207–237, 1969.

MANNION, L., An Investigation into the Process of Teacher Socialisation, PhD dissertation, School of Research in Education, University of Bradford, 1974.

BEHAVING IN ORGANIZATIONS

Most of us spend a considerable part of our lives as members of a variety of organizations. Modern man, it has been said, is *man in organizations* (Blau and Scott, 1963). During the last decade the growing interest in what has commonly been referred to as 'organization theory' is indicative of the need to understand the nature of organizations, their differing internal structures and operations, and the differing demands that they make upon the individuals who comprise them.

To a large extent the way in which a member of an organization behaves depends upon the nature and the purpose of the particular organization. Behaviour appropriate to and expected of a member of a religious organization is different from that expected of the same person in a political, recreational, or educational setting. Depending upon the nature and purpose of the organization there are differences in the ways in which authority is exercised in the regulation of one organization member's behaviour towards another. Experiment 5, 'a study of expectations for individuals in different organizations', brought into operation five types of power in terms of which one individual exercises authority over another. The original contribution of French and Raven (1959) in distinguishing between reward, coercive, legitimate, expert, and referent power was applied to two very different types of organizations (schools and factories). In the case of the school, it was the relationship between the regular class teacher and the student on school practice which was examined; in the case of the factory it was the sandwich course student's relationship ' with his industry-based supervisor to which attention was directed. Whilst in both organizations the student/supervisor relationships were similarly structured, the 'normative' nature of the school as an organization as compared with the 'remunerative' nature of the factory suggested that differences might exist in the bases of power governing supervisor/student relationships.

Experiment 6 'role conflict' explored the role of the student as a member of an educational organization. 'Role' refers to the expected behaviour associated with a position within a social group. The student position, it was held, is associated with a range of expected behaviours, expected that is, not only by the incumbents (the students) themselves, but also by those occupying counter-positions to them — lecturers, personal tutors, parents, boy-friends and girl-friends. When the student perceives differing and incompatible expectations for his behaviour arising out of his relationships with counter-position occupants, the term 'role-conflict' appropriately describes the structuring of those relation-ships from the student's point of view. To what degree such perceived role conflict causes actual discomfort to the student will depend upon a number of factors not the least of which is the *legitimacy* of his role partners' expectations for his behaviour and their varying abilities to *sanction* him and his own reaction to such pressures in the light of his unique psychological make-up. This last point, the degree to which one is able to predict conflict or clash of interest in social settings arising out of the interplay of organizational demands and individual needs, is the subject material of Experiment 7 'self identities and behaviour in organizations'.

Self-identities, in part composed of self-ability ratings, beliefs, attitudes, and values are being formed during the years which precede entry into higher education. It is at university or college, however, as university students or college students, that relatively 'backstage' beliefs and attitudes are crystallized out into manifestly 'front-stage' self-identities. These, as has been shown in the experiment, enable one to predict a considerable part of the students' acitivities. In the experiment, for example, the social-intellectual and the social-fun role orientations appear to be formed and maintained through the close and continuous association of undergraduates with their fellow students; the very opposite seems to hold for the academic and vocational self identities.

The impact that universities and colleges have upon their student populations is as yet relatively unexplored in the UK. Experiment 7 and 'the study of the need for achievement' (in the section on individual differences on p. 161) suggest two of many possible personal attributes which illuminate student behaviour and accomplishment in educational settings.

References

BLAU, P. M., and SCOTT, W. R., Formal Organizations, London, Routledge and Kegan Paul, 1963.

BOLTON, C. D. and KAMMEYER, K. C. W., The University Student: a Study of Student Behavior and Values. New Haven: Connecticut College and University Press, 1967.

COHEN, L., Functional Dependence, Exchanges and Power of Influence. *International Journal of Educational Sciences,* 3, 1, 47–51, 1969.

COHEN, L., Students' Perceptions of the School Practice Period. *Research in Education,* **2**, 52–58, 1969.

COHEN, L. and SCAIFE, R., Self-environment Similarity and Satisfaction in a College of Education. *Human Relations,* **26**, 1, 1973.

FINLAYSON, D. S. and COHEN, L., The Teacher's Role: A Comparative Study of the Conceptions of College of Education Students and Headteachers. *British Journal of Educational Psychology,* **37**, 1, 22–31, 1967.

FRENCH, J. R. P. and RAVEN, B. H., The Bases of Social Power. In *CARTWRIGHT, D.* (Ed), *Studies in Social Powers.* Ann Arbor: Michigan, University of Michigan Press, 1959, pp. 118–149.

GETZELS, J. W., Conflict and Role Behavior in the Educational Setting, in *W. W. CHARTERS and N. L. GAGE* (eds), *Readings in the Social Psychology of Education,* Allyn and Bacon, pp. 309–318, 1963.

KAHN, R. L., WOLFE, D. M., QUINN, R. P., SNOEK, J. D., and ROSENTHAL, R. A., Organizational Stress: Studies in Role Conflict and Ambiguity. N.Y., John Wiley and Sons, 1964.

KELSALL, R. K. and KELSALL, H. M., The School Teacher in England and the United States. London: Pergamon Press, 1969, pp. 52–66.

McLEISH, J., Students' Attitudes and College Environments. Cambridge: Institute of Education, 1970.

VALUE SYSTEMS OF OCCUPATIONAL GROUPS

Aim

To explore the association between value systems and occupational choice.

Method

Samples of different occupational groups, or, in the case of students, intending-occupational groups, complete the Rokeach Terminal and Instrumental Values Surveys.

Analysis

Differences in the mean ranking of values between various occupational groups may be tested using the Kruskal—Wallis one way analysis of variance (see Appendix 2, Treatment 6, p. 202).

The Value Survey Instrument

Terminal values are ranked before instrumental values as follows.

Terminal Values

To a large extent the choices a person makes in life, (choices to do with his career, friends, way of life, etc.) reflect the values that he holds as important to him. We would like you to rank a number of value statements in *their order of importance to you*. Among other things we wish to explore the relationship between values and the choice of careers in industry, business, teaching, and nursing.

In the Table 1:23 below, please put a '1' next to the value that you consider to be most important, a '2' next to the value which is second most important, etc. Go on ranking the value statements until the value you consider least important relative to the others is ranked '18'.

Table 1:23

Terminal values	Rank
A comfortable life (*a prosperous life*)	
An exciting life (*a stimulating, active life*)	
A sense of accomplishment (*lasting contribution*)	
A world at peace (*free of war and conflict*)	
A world of beauty (*beauty of nature and the arts*)	
Equality (*brotherhood, equal opportunity for all*)	
Family security (*taking care of loved ones*)	
Freedom (*independence, free choice*)	
Happiness (*contentedness*)	
Inner harmony (*freedom from inner conflict*)	
Mature love (*sexual and spiritual intimacy*)	
National security (*protection from attack*)	
Pleasure (*an enjoyable, leisurely life*)	
Salvation (*saved, eternal life*)	
Self-respect (*self-esteem*)	
Social recognition (*respect, admiration*)	
True friendship (*close companionship*)	
Wisdom (*a mature understanding of life*)	

Instrumental Values

Now do the same with the statements of values listed in Table 1:24. Put a '1' next to the value that you consider to be most important, a '2' next to the value which is second most important, etc.

Table 1:24

Instrumental Values	Rank
Ambitious (*hard-working, aspiring*)	
Broadminded (*open-minded*)	
Capable (*competent, effective*)	
Cheerful (*lighthearted, joyful*)	
Clean (*neat, tidy*)	
Courageous (*standing up for your beliefs*)	
Forgiving (*willing to pardon others*)	
Helpful (*working for the welfare of others*)	
Honest (*sincere, truthful*)	
Imaginative (*daring, creative*)	
Independent (*self-reliant, self-sufficient*)	
Intellectual (*intelligent, reflective*)	
Logical (*consistent, rational*)	
Loving (*affectionate, tender*)	
Obedient (*dutiful, respectful*)	
Polite (*courteous, well-mannered*)	
Responsible (*dependable, reliable*)	
Self-controlled (*restrained, self-disciplined*)	

By way of example the terminal values rankings of 6 male student teachers, 31 male social studies undergraduates intending careers in Social Work, and 58 male undergraduates reading Business and Management Studies are examined below (see Appendix 2, Treatment 2, p. 191 for the computation of median rankings from raw data).

Table 1:25

Median Rankings of Terminal Values in Intending Teaching, Social Work, and Business student groups.

Terminal Value	Teachers		Social Workers		Businessmen	
	Median	Rank	Median	Rank	Median	Rank
A comfortable life	11.83	35	14.55	43	5.29	4
An exciting life	14.61	44	12.61	38	7.11	13
Sense accomplishment	5.22	3	6.59	11	9.58	30
Peace	7.85	17	9.20	27	9.22	28
Beauty	8.89	25	9.34	29	15.89	48
Equality	9.18	26	8.51	24	16.11	50
Security	5.72	6	14.81	45	10.07	31
Freedom	6.32	10	6.29	9	14.05	42
Happiness	7.91	18	12.21	36	13.82	40
Inner harmony	7.40	15	8.01	19	15.01	46
Mature love	6.65	12	8.11	20	13.91	41
National security	6.14	8	10.94	33	12.45	37
Pleasure	13.21	39	16.03	49	8.52	23
Salvation	16.39	52	16.47	53	16.30	51
Self-respect	7.82	16	7.28	14	15.83	47
Social recognition	8.48	22	16.78	54	10.49	32
True friendship	5.38	5	6.01	7	11.11	34
Wisdom	5.02	1	5.13	2	8.33	21
	$R_1 = 354$		$R_2 = 513$		$R_3 = 618$	

Differences are tested by the Kruskal–Wallis test (see Appendix 2, Treatment 6, p. 202). In the above example, a value of 7.91 indicates that the differences in the rank ordering of terminal values by future teachers, social workers, and businessmen is significant and could have occurred by chance only 25 times in a 1000. If we examine Table 1:25 more closely it is at once apparent that there are very large differences in the ranking of the three groups on certain terminal values such as 'a comfortable life' and 'an exciting life'. We could, if we wished, examine the significance of the differences between the three aspiring-occupational groups on these two values (or any other grouping of values) by means of the Kruskal–Wallis one-way analysis of variance (see Rokeach, 1968; Feather, 1970). Supposing, however, that we are interested in the significance of the difference in the ranking of the future teachers and future social workers on only one terminal value, for example, 'a comfortable life'.

From Table 1:25 we see that the future teachers' median score on 'a comfortable life' is 11.83 (ranked 35) and the future social workers' median score is 14.55 (ranked 43). The question we wish to pose is: 'Do future teachers rank "a comfortable life" significantly higher than future social workers?' The median test (Appendix 2, Treatment 15) is an appropriate statistic by which to test the difference in the ranking of 'a comfortable life' by the two groups. To perform the median test we must first put the teaching and social work groups together and obtain the *median score of all scores* in the combined sample. Both sets of scores are then dichotomized at the combined median and these data are then cast in a 2 x 2 table as in Table 1:26 below (see Appendix 2, Treatment 2, p. 191 for calculation of median and Appendix 2, Treatment 7, p. 205 for chi-square in 2 x 2 contingency tables). The combined median score of future teachers and social workers on 'a comfortable life' = 13.71.

Table 1:26

	Future teachers	Future Social workers	
Scores below combined median (i.e. higher ranking)	A 40	B 11	A + B 51
Scores above combined median (i.e. lower ranking)	C 21	D 20	C + D 41
	A + C 61	B + D 31	N = 92

$$\chi^2 = \frac{N\left(|AD - BC| - \dfrac{N}{2}\right)^2}{(A + B)(C + D)(A + C)(B + D)} \quad \text{d.f.} = 1$$

$$\chi^2 = \frac{92(|800 - 231| - 46)^2}{(51 \times 41 \times 61 \times 31)} = 6.36$$

$$\chi^2 = 6.36 \quad \text{d.f.} = 1 \quad p < 0.05$$

We conclude that in our sample future teachers rank 'a comfortable life' significantly more highly than future social workers.

Table 1:27

Median Rankings of Terminal Values for _____ , _____ , and Occupational Groups

Terminal Value	$(n = $ $)$ Median Rank	$(n = $ $)$ Median Rank	$(n = $ $)$ Median Rank
A comfortable life			
An exciting life			
Sense accomplishment			
Peace			
Beauty			
Equality			
Security			
Freedom			
Happiness			
Inner harmony			
Mature love			
National security			
Pleasure			
Salvation			
Self-respect			
Social recognition			
True friendship			
Wisdom			
	$R_1 = $ _____	$R_2 = $ _____	$R_3 = $ _____

$$H = \frac{12}{N(N+1)} \frac{R_j^2}{n_j} - 3(N+1)$$

$$= \underline{\hspace{3cm}} \quad \underline{\hspace{0.8cm}} + \underline{\hspace{0.8cm}} + \underline{\hspace{0.8cm}} \quad - 3(\quad + 1)$$

$$= \underline{\hspace{3cm}}$$

Interpret your findings briefly below.

_____

_____

_____

_____

_____

A comparison of the rank ordering of terminal value _____ by the
two occupational groups _____ and _____

1   Combined median of both samples = _____

Table 1:28
Occupational Groups   _____   _____

Scores below combined median (i.e. higher ranking)	A	B	A + B
Scores above combined median (i.e. lower ranking)	C	D	C + D
	A + C	B + D	N =

$$\chi^2 = \frac{N\left(|AD - BC| - \frac{N}{2}\right)^2}{(A+B)(C+D)(A+C)(B+D)} = \text{d.f.} = 1$$

$$\chi^2 = \underline{\hspace{3cm}}$$

$$= \underline{\hspace{3cm}}$$

Interpret your findings briefly below.

_____

_____

_____

Table 1:29

**Median Rankings of Instrumental Values for   ,   , and
      Occupational Groups**

Instrumental Value	$(n = \quad)$ Median Rank	$(n = \quad)$ Median Rank	$(n = \quad)$ Median Rank
Ambitious			
Broad-minded			
Capable			
Cheerful			
Clean			
Courageous			
Forgiving			
Helpful			
Honest			
Imaginative			
Independent			
Intellectual			
Logical			
Loving			
Obedient			
Polite			
Responsible			
Self-controlled			
	$R_1 = \underline{\quad\quad}$	$R_2 = \underline{\quad\quad}$	$R_3 = \underline{\quad\quad}$

$$H = \frac{12}{N(N+1)} \frac{R_j^2}{n_j} - 3(N+1)$$

$$= \underline{\hspace{2cm}} \quad \underline{\hspace{1cm}} + \underline{\hspace{1cm}} + \underline{\hspace{1cm}} - 3(\quad + 1)$$

$$= \underline{\hspace{3cm}}$$

Interpret your findings briefly below.

_____

_____

_____

_____

_____

A comparison of the rank ordering of instrumental value _____ by the two occupational groups _____ and _____ .

1   Combined median of both samples = _____

Table 1:30
Occupational groups

	_____	_____	
Scores below combined median (i.e. higher ranking)	A	B	A + B
Scores above combined median (i.e. lower ranking)	C	D	C + D
	A + C	B + D	N =

$$\chi^2 = \frac{N \left(|AD - BC| - \frac{N}{2} \right)^2}{(A + B)(C + D)(A + C)(B + D)} \quad \text{d.f.} = 1$$

$$\chi^2 = \underline{\hspace{3cm}}$$

$$= \underline{\hspace{3cm}}$$

Interpret your findings briefly below.

_____

_____

_____

Further Applications

1   Within any occupational group (for example, teachers, social workers, librarians) examine the differences in the terminal and the instrumental values of males and females. Discuss your findings with male and female representatives of these occupational groups.

2   Rokeach (1969) has explored value systems in relation to religion. Design a study to explore differences in the terminal values of three religious faiths or denominations.

3   How is age related to differences in value systems within any occupational group?

References

FEATHER, N. T., Educational Choice and Student Attitudes in Relation to Terminal and Instrumental Values, *Australian Journal of Psychology*, 22, 2, pp. 127–143, 1970.
ROKEACH, M., A Theory of Organization and Change within Value-Attitude Systems, *Journal of Social Issues*, 24, 1, pp. 13–33, 1968.
ROKEACH, M., Value Systems in Religion, *Review of Religious Research*, 11, pp. 3–23, 1969.

STUDENTS' ATTITUDES TO THEIR COURSE

Aim

To evaluate the use of an experimental approach in a course on memory in terms of the favourability/unfavourability of students' assessments.

Method

Pre-test*. All students are asked to rate the concept, the Psychology of Memory Course, on a 25-item semantic differential scale before being randomly-assigned to (experimental) 'E' and (control) 'C' groups. The lecturer acts as tutor to both groups during the experiment. *The control group* receives a 3-week course consisting of three lectures on memory together with assigned readings. *The experimental group* receives the same work (i.e. content) but in the form of three experiments in which the students participate as subjects. Each experiment is followed by group discussion and the compilation of a short report on the major findings of the experiment together with their implications.

Post-test. E and C groups again rate the concept, the Psychology of Memory Course, on the 25-item semantic differential scale at the end of the 3-week period.

Evaluation Questionnaire (pre-test wording in brackets)

We would like you to rate part of your current course in psychology by means of the adjectival scales below. If, for example, you were asked to rate *the psychology of memory* section of the course and you thought it was (going to be) very complex you would place a cross at the complex end of the scale complex-easy, thus:

complex   : X :__:__:__:__:__:__ : easy

If, on the other hand, you thought the course was (going to be) very easy, you would put a cross thus:

complex   :__:__:__:__:__:__: X : easy

If your judgments were less extreme you would use the intermediate points on the scale. Use the middle position if you have no feelings either way.

---

*It should be stressed that in the pre-test evaluation students are asked to anticipate what the course will be like. The pre-test version of the evaluative questionnaire has specially-adapted wording.

The Psychology of Memory Course

Useful	:__:__:__:__:__:__:	Useless
Dull	:__:__:__:__:__:__:	Exciting
Interesting	:__:__:__:__:__:__:	Uninteresting
Unimportant	:__:__:__:__:__:__:	Important
Good	:__:__:__:__:__:__:	Bad
Well-taught	:__:__:__:__:__:__:	Badly-taught
Positive	:__:__:__:__:__:__:	Negative
Relevant	:__:__:__:__:__:__:	Irrelevant
Successfully-learned	:__:__:__:__:__:__:	Unsuccessfully-learned
Professionally necessary	:__:__:__:__:__:__:	Professionally unnecessary
Advantageous	:__:__:__:__:__:__:	Disadvantageous
Worth while	:__:__:__:__:__:__:	Worthless
Applicable	:__:__:__:__:__:__:	Inapplicable
Boring	:__:__:__:__:__:__:	Enjoyable
Uninspired	:__:__:__:__:__:__:	Inspiring
Sound	:__:__:__:__:__:__:	Unsound
Practical	:__:__:__:__:__:__:	Impractical
Purposeless	:__:__:__:__:__:__:	Purposeful
Appropriate	:__:__:__:__:__:__:	Inappropriate
Excellent	:__:__:__:__:__:__:	Poor
Unrewarding	:__:__:__:__:__:__:	Rewarding
Well-spent	:__:__:__:__:__:__:	Ill-spent
Profitable	:__:__:__:__:__:__:	Unprofitable
Not valuable	:__:__:__:__:__:__:	Valuable
Suitable	:__:__:__:__:__:__:	Unsuitable

Analysis

By means of an adaptation of the McNemar test for the significance of change (a full explanation of the procedures and computation is given in Appendix 2, Treatment 11, pp. 212–213).

Directions

1 Take each group (experimentals and controls) separately.

2 Assign seven to the favourable pole of each semantic differential scale and one to the unfavourable pole.

3 For each adjectival scale construct a matrix by which to identify each student's rating before and after the memory course. By way of illustration the hypothetical before-and-after ratings of two subjects have been entered in the matrix below. The first student considered the course quite useful (rating 5) before the work took place and increased his rating to 6 as a result of the experimental course. We enter the matrix at 'before' position 5 and put a tally in the cell where 'before 5' intersects with 'after 6'. The second student was not very favourable before rating 2 and was even less impressed after the experience 1. Again, the tally is placed at the intersection of 'before 2' and 'after 1'.

Table 1:31

		Before						
		Useful					Useless	
		7	6	5	4	3	2	1
Useful	7							
	6							
	5							
After	4							
	3							
	2							
Useless	1							

4 Repeat for each student.

5 Use the McNemar test for the significance of change to test the significance and the direction of changes in the before-and-after ratings on each adjectival scale. Enter these as you compute them in Tables 1:32 and 1:33 below.

Table 1:32
Experimental Group Changes

Adjectival pair	More favourable	Less favourable	No change
Useful—useless			
Dull—exciting			
Interesting—uninteresting			
Unimportant—important			
Good—bad			
Well-taught—badly-taught			
Positive—negative			
Relevant—irrelevant			
Successfully-learned—unsuccessfully-learned			
Professionally necessary—professionally unnecessary			
Advantageous—disadvantageous			
Worth while—worthless			
Applicable—inapplicable			
Boring—enjoyable			
Uninspired—inspiring			
Sound—unsound			
Practical—impractical			
Purposeless—purposeful			
Appropriate—inappropriate			
Excellent—poor			
Unrewarding—rewarding			
Well-spent—ill-spent			
Profitable—unprofitable			
Not valuable—valuable			
Suitable—unsuitable			

Totals

Use the following conventions to record the significance of the change on each adjectival pair:

$$* = p < 0.05$$
$$** = p < 0.01$$

Table 1:33
Control Group Changes

Adjectival pair	More favourable	Less favourable	No change
Useful—useless			
Dull—exciting			
Interesting—Uninteresting			
Unimportant—important			
Good—bad			
Well-taught—badly-taught			
Positive—negative			
Relevant—irrelevant			
Successfully-learned—unsuccessfully-learned			
Professionally necessary—professionally unnecessary			
Advantageous—disadvantageous			
Worth while—worthless			
Applicable—inapplicable			
Boring—enjoyable			
Uninspired—inspiring			
Sound—unsound			
Practical—impractical			
Purposeless—purposeful			
Appropriate—inappropriate			
Excellent—poor			
Unrewarding—rewarding			
Well-spent—ill-spent			
Profitable—unprofitable			
Not valuable—valuable			
Suitable—unsuitable			
Totals			

Use the following conventions to record the significance of the change on each adjectival pair:

$$* = p < 0.05$$
$$** = p < 0.01$$

Briefly, interpret the differences between the results in Table 1:32 (experimental group changes) and those in Table 1:33 (control group changes) below.

_____

_____

_____

_____

_____

_____

_____

_____

Suppose that in Table 1:32, out of 25 adjectival scales, the experimental group change is found to be 20 in the direction of more favourable and 5 in the direction of less favourable. Are we justified in concluding that overall, the experimental group changes significantly in the direction of greater favourability? Look at Appendix 2, Treatment 12, p. 214 for the application of the binomial test in the resolution of this particular question.

Further Applications

The experimental design for measuring changes in attitudes may be employed in the evaluation of any type of activity. Students may wish to examine changing attitudes (using the adaptation of the McNemar test for the significance of change) without recourse to a matched control group. For example, using the Oliver and Butcher Manchester Opinion Scales in Education (Oliver and Butcher, 1962)* how do student teachers' attitudes change in respect of naturalism, tendermindedness, and radicalism, over the school practice period or over the course of a year? Scores on each of these sub-scales might be broken down as follows. Take, for example, tendermindedness:

---

*The Manchester Opinion Scales in Education (Oliver and Butcher, 1962) are obtainable from the Department of Education, University of Manchester.

Table 1:34 Changes in tendermindedness

Before

	Very high	High	Average	Low	Very low
Very high					
High					
Average					
Low					
Very low					

After

Students may wish to examine overall change in attitudes during the school practice period in two groups of subjects — those who report having experienced severe discipline problems and those not experiencing any discipline problems during their work in schools.

Reference

OLIVER, R. A. C. and BUTCHER, H. J., Teachers' Attitudes to Education: The Structure of Educational Attitudes, *British Journal of Social and Clinical Psychology*, 1, pp. 56–59, 1962.

VALUING

The effectiveness of a course of study is often judged by the degree to which pupils or students are able to demonstrate their acquisition of the academic content that has constituted a series of lessons or lectures. Another important element in judging effectiveness, however, is the favourability or unfavourability of the attitudes that a course of study generates in its recipients. Experiment 9 provided a way of judging the favourability of students' attitudes towards a particular teaching method. The longitudinal design of the experiment allows the researcher to measure changes in attitudes occurring over a short period of time. Whilst *attitudes* are relatively more enduring than *opinions* they are less permanent than *values*.

Values may be distinguished from attitudes in terms of their depth, permanence and comprehensiveness. Values are concerned both with 'modes of conduct' and with 'end-states of existence' (Rokeach, 1968). That is to say, values underpin an individual's on-going behaviour as he pursues those goals or ends which he firmly believes are preferable to others.

In Experiment 8, 'value systems of occupational groups', two different sets of values were distinguished, *terminal* values (representing ends or goals) and *instrumental* values (representing behaviour towards those ends). Rokeach has suggested that a terminal value can be identified when a word or a phrase can be meaningfully inserted into a sentence such as: 'I believe that . . .' (such and such an end-state of existence, e.g. salvation, or wisdom) 'is personally and socially worth striving for'. An instrumental value can be identified when a word or phrase can be meaningfully inserted in a sentence such as: 'I believe that . . .' (such and such a mode of conduct, e.g. honesty, self-respect, or courage, etc.) 'is personally and socially preferable in all situations with respect to all objects'. The relationship between terminal and instrumental values may be clarified as follows. To attain the end-state of wisdom, for example, may require ongoing behaviour in which an individual exhibits *inter alia*, honesty, self-respect, and courage. Instrumental values, as their nomenclature implies, are employed in the pursuit and attainment of terminal values. If terminal values 'guide' ongoing behaviour it ought to be possible to select various examples of such behaviour (occupational choice, for example) in order to explore how such choice might be associated with an individual's declared goals in life. Experiment 8 attempted precisely that. In line with a hypothesized association between value systems and occupational choice, it was expected that 'people orientated' professions (Rosenberg, 1957) such as teaching or social work would attract individuals for whom terminal values such as 'a sense of accomplishment' and instrumental values such as 'helpful' would rank higher than in 'extrinsic-reward orientated' professions such as business and industrial management, where the likelihood of 'a comfortable life' and 'ambition', being more highly valued, would be congruent with the choice of such occupations. Broadly, the results in the experiment lent support to such proposed relationships.

Valuing is one important way in which man imposes a system of priorities upon his social environment enabling him to effect choices and control social outcomes. As in Overview 1 we come again to the recurring theme of man striving to introduce order and thus *meaning* into the social environment.

References

ASPIN, D., On the 'Educated' Person and the Problem of Values in Teacher Education and Training, in *LOMAX, D.,* (Ed.), *The Education of Teachers in Britain,* John Wiley, London, pp. 193—217, 1973.

FEATHER, N. T., Value Systems and Education: The Flinders Programme of Value Research, *The Australian Journal of Education,* **16,** 2, pp. 136—149, 1972.

FEATHER, N. T., Educational Choice and Student Attitudes in Relation to Terminal and Instrumental Values, *Australian Journal of Psychology,* **22,** 2, pp. 127—143, 1970.

KELVIN, P., The Bases of Social Behaviour, Holt, Rinehart and Winston, London, Chap. 2, 1969.

KERLINGER, F. N., Foundations of Behavioral Research, Holt, Rinehart and Winston, London, Chap. 15—17, 1970.

ROKEACH, M., Beliefs, Attitudes and Values, Jossey-Bass, San Francisco, 1968.

ROKEACH, M., The Nature of Human Values, Free-Press—Macmillan, New York, 1973.

ROKEACH, M., MILLER, M. G. and SNYDER, J. A., The Value Gap between Police and Policed, *Journal of Social Issues,* **27,** 2, pp. 155—171, 1971.

ROSENBERG, M., Occupations and Values, Glencoe: The Free Press, 1957.

RECALL AND RECOGNITION

Aim

To compare the extent to which a list of syllables can be recalled without cue, or recognized from a list of alternatives.

Materials

Sufficient copies of List A for all subjects, copies of List B for half of the subjects, and blank paper for the other half and pencils.

Method

Subjects are randomly divided into Group 1 (for recognition task) and Group 2 (for recall task). *They should not be told to which group they belong.* All subjects are first given List A, which consists of ten nonsense syllables in consonant-vowel-consonant form. Nonsense syllables have the form of simple word-stimuli, but as they have no meaning they are less likely to be influenced by their familiarity or relevance to the subject. On presentation of the list the experimenter says: 'Before you is a list of nonsense syllables. You will be given two minutes in which to memorize them. Start now.' After 2 minutes the experimenter says: 'Stop. Please put the sheet out of sight.' Group 1 is then given List B, which contains the words from List A interspersed with 20 new syllables. Subjects are asked to underline those which were in the original list. Group 2 is given a sheet of paper and asked to write down the syllables which were on List A, in any order.

List A	List B	
JID	RUY	FEP
XAZ	BIW	JUL
QUG	NER	JID
MEP	MEP	FYM
LUJ	QUG	XAZ
RUY	SUW	DOJ
NEJ	QEC	FIW
WOC	NIZ	LUJ
VUK	XIH	VOF
DIB	SOQ	NEJ
	DIB	JOF
	VUK	TEB
	KES	XAD
	WOC	MUH
	KOV	SEH

Analysis

One mark is given for each syllable correctly recalled or recognized. Raw scores are entered on the result sheet. Comparison of the mean score for each group will give some indication of the relative extents of recall and recognition. Statistical estimation of the chances of such differences occurring accidently is by means of the t test (Appendix 2, Treatment 4(b), p. 197).

Raw Scores

Table 1:35

Group 1 (recall)	Group 2 (recognition)
2	9
4	8
8	9
2	8
7	8
6	4
7	7
7	10

$n = 8$ $n = 8$
$\bar{X} = 5.38$ $\bar{X} = 7.87$
$\Sigma X = 43$ $\Sigma X = 63$
$\Sigma X^2 = 271$ $\Sigma X^2 = 519$

From the analysis a value of 2.35 for t is obtained. This is significant at the 0.05 level, i.e. there is less than one chance in 20 that such differences between groups will occur by chance. It is therefore concluded that there is a difference in the amount of learned material which a subject can recall and recognize.

Raw Scores

Table 1:36

Group 1 (recall)	Group 2 (recognition)

$n =$ $n =$

$\bar{X} =$ $\bar{X} =$

$\Sigma X =$ $\Sigma X =$

$\Sigma X^2 =$ $\Sigma X^2 =$

Summary

Both recall and recognition are important features of memory. The experiment demonstrated that subjects are able to recognize considerably greater quantities of material than they can recall without any cue. It must therefore be assumed that the subjects actually retained quite a lot of the stimuli syllables in their memories, but for many of them they did not have an adequate means of retrieving them from the store.

Investigating problems of memory is not, then, simply concerned with determining how much material is retained under a given set of circumstances, but also with how much of the stored material is available to the subject, and by what means.

What are the implications of this study for teachers using essay-type and multiple-choice questions in examinations? Does guessing influence these two modes of response to the same extent? What would be the effect of offering subjects a second list which did not include any of the original stimuli syllables but did include ten which were very similar?

References

DAVIS, R., SUTHERLAND, N. S. & JUDD, B., Information Content in Recognition and Recall, *Journal of Experimental Psychology*, 61, pp. 422–428, 1961.
POSTMAN, L. & RAU, L., Retention as a Function of the Method of Measurement, *University of California Publications in Psychology*, 8, pp. 217–270, 1957.

SERIAL RECALL

Aim

To determine the serial positions of those items in a word list which are most readily recalled.

Materials

List of words. Blank test papers and pencils for all subjects.

Method

All subjects perform this task in the same way. To commence the experiment say to the subjects: 'I am going to read aloud a list of words. Listen carefully to them and try to memorize them so that you can recall them, in any order.'

The words from the word list are then read aloud in a clear voice, with a pause of 2 seconds between each. When the list is completed the blank test-papers are distributed and subjects are told: 'Write down the words you have just heard. You may write them in any order. You have 45 seconds in which to do this.'

Analysis

To score the test responses the experimenter reads out each word from the list in turn. At each word all the subjects who have correctly recalled it raise their hands and a count is taken. One mark is given for each correctly recalled word. The total for each word is entered on the result sheet, and the percentage recall rate for the whole group calculated.

Word List

PIG	BOX	TAP
HAT	ROT	
ROD	DOG	
SIN	FEW	
FAT	GAS	
CAR	POD	

Table 1:37
Test sheet

No. in group = 19

Position	1	2	3	4	5	6	7	8	9	10	11	12	13
No. correct responses	19	17	16	10	11	5	6	7	6	9	10	13	13
Recall rate (%)	100	89	84	53	58	26	32	37	32	47	53	68	68

Figure 1:7
Percentage Recall Rate Against Serial Position

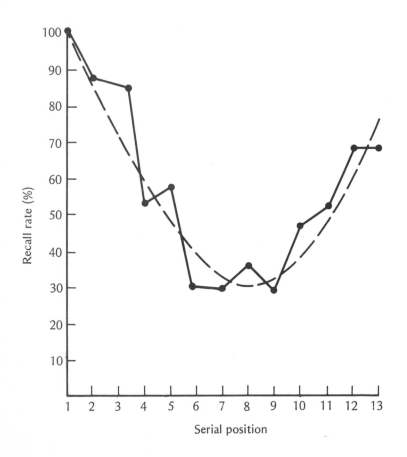

Table 1:38
Test sheet

No. in group =

Position	1	2	3	4	5	6	7	8	9	10	11	12	13
No. correct responses													
Recall rate (%)													

Figure 1:8
Percentage Recall Rate Against Serial Position

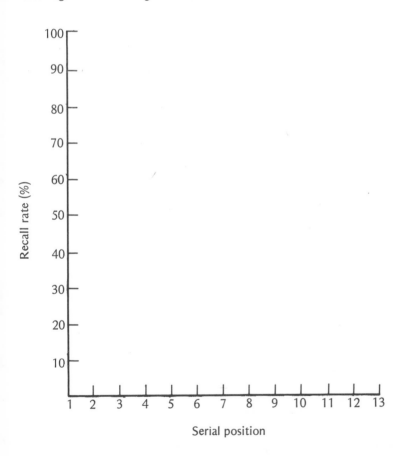

Summary

The graph in the analysis shows two curves. That produced by joining together the actual points which were plotted is irregular. Each time a group of subjects perform this experiment there will be different irregularities. The graph will usually show the same overall tendency however, and that is illustrated by the 'ideal' curve which has been drawn in as a dotted line. The experiment demonstrated that items at the beginning and end of a series were more readily recalled than those in the middle. This is thought to be due to two different effects, sometimes referred to as the 'primacy' and 'recency' effects.

Modern theorists postulate two different memory stores, a short-term store (STS) and a long-term store (LTS). Items registered by the subject's senses are placed immediately in the STS. This has a very limited capacity, possibly only two or three items at a time. After a short period of time this STS decays and, unless the items have been transferred to the LTS they will be forgotten. The LTS is seen as a relatively permanent store of material, though subjects may not always have the ability to retrieve it when they require it.

From the graph it is possible to see the effects of these two processes. Items recalled from the early portion of the list are obtained from the LTS. Items further down the list were less successfully stored and recall rates had diminished. The last three or four items were more successfully recalled because they were still available in STS. From your own data and 'ideal' curve:

1   Estimate the mean number of items held in the LTS by assuming that the early drop in recall continued.

2   Estimate the mean number of items in STS by the same process.

3   How much individual difference was there between the most and least successful recall scores in the group? Was the difference largely in STS or LTS?

4   What would be the effect of substituting the experimenter's name for item 7 or item 8 in the list?

5   Did members of the group adopt particular strategies to aid recall?

References

DEESE, J., & KAUFMAN, R. A., Serial Effects in Recall of Unorganized and Sequentially Organized Verbal Material, *Journal of Experimental Psychology*, 54, pp. 180–187, 1957.
GLANZER, M., & CUNITZ, A. R., Two Storage Mechanisms in Free Recall, *Journal of Verbal Learning and Verbal Behaviour*, 5, pp. 351–360, 1966.

EXPERIMENT 12

RETROACTIVE AND PROACTIVE INHIBITION

Aim

To examine possible effects upon the recall of a word list of another word list learned:

1 before it.
2 after it.

Materials

Sufficient copies of Lists 1 and 2 on p. 119 for the subjects (half of them will require one list and half the other), pencils and paper for test, and any printed sheets for vowel cancellation.

Method

Subjects are randomly assigned to one of four groups. Groups 1 and 2 will investigate proactive inhibition and Groups 3 and 4 will investigate retroactive inhibition. *They must not be told this.* The plan of the experiment is that Groups 1 and 3 are experimental groups. Each learns two lists of words and then has to recall either the first list or the second. Groups 2 and 4 act as control groups. As they learn only one list it is necessary to give them a simple, relatively mechanical task to occupy them. This particularly applies to Group 4 which will have learned its list and may engage in rehearsal. Vowel cancellation is used for this purpose. Two 10-minute learning sessions followed by a test are arranged on the following schedule:

	First Session (10 min)	Second Session (10 min)	Test
Group 1	List 1	List 2	List 2
Group 2	Vowel cancellation	List 2	List 2
Group 3	List 1	List 2	List 1
Group 4	List 1	Vowel cancellation	List 1

When the groups have been allocated, List 1 should be placed, face down, in front of each member of Groups 1, 3 and 4. They are told: 'Before you is a list of words. You are to commit them to memory by any means you choose, providing it does not interfere with the work of others. Learn the list so that you can recall it in any order. You have 10 minutes.

Group 2 are given printed sheets and told: 'Work through this sheet crossing out all the vowels. Work as quickly as you can without missing any out. You have 10 minutes.'

After the first session let the groups rest for a few minutes and then proceed with the second session. After the second session the groups are tested on recall, according to the schedule. Subjects are given one mark for each correctly recalled word.

Analysis

The result sheet should summarize the raw scores for each group. Comparison of Group 1 scores — those subjects who learned a list prior to the one on which they were tested — with Group 2 scores — subjects who were simply kept busy for 10 minutes — will show whether proactive inhibition has occurred. Calculation of the mean score for each group will give some indication, but to determine whether any difference is greater than that to be expected purely by chance, a t test is used (see Appendix 2, Treatment 4(b), p. 197). A similar analysis of scores for Groups 3 and 4 will determine whether retroactive inhibition has taken place.

Table 1:39
Raw Scores for All Groups

Group 1	Group 2	Group 3	Group 4
18	20	13	19
13	20	10	19
18	19	16	19
20	18	9	20
17	14	12	16
20	12	19	20
15	19	17	20
20	13	14	20
6	19	15	20
19			

$n = 10$	$n = 9$	$n = 9$	$n = 9$
$\bar{X} = 16.6$	$\bar{X} = 17.11$	$\bar{X} = 13.89$	$\bar{X} = 19.22$
$\Sigma X = 166.0$	$\Sigma X = 154.0$	$\Sigma X = 125.0$	$\Sigma X = 173.0$
$\Sigma X^2 = 2928.0$	$\Sigma X^2 = 2716.0$	$\Sigma X^2 = 1821.0$	$\Sigma X^2 = 3339.0$

t Test — Groups 1 & 2

$t = 0.82f$ not significant   d.f. = 17

Whilst there was a small difference between the mean scores of the two groups this could easily have occurred by chance. It is therefore assumed that this experiment found no effect which could be ascribed to proactive inhibition.

t Test — Groups 3 & 4

$t = 2.73$ $p < 0.01$ d.f. = 16

(one-tailed test of significance; see glossary, p. 235).

As might have been expected from the difference in means, there is less than one chance in 20 that the differences between groups is a chance occurrence. It is therefore concluded that retroactive inhibition has taken place.

Note:

If the subjects are to re-convene within 48 hours, the test of recall should be repeated. It is often found that by this time the effects of proactive inhibition are much more marked.

List 1		List 2	
ANXIOUS	MUTE	CARELESS	BLITHE
CONFESS	UNIFORM	COLD	MOTLEY
CURIOUS	SHAKY	MEAGRE	SALIENT
VIRTUOUS	MASSIVE	CALM	DANGEROUS
CRAFTY	EAGER	PROSPEROUS	DIRECT
FRANK	RUDE	RELIABLE	LOUD
SLEEK	RUINOUS	PETULANT	MUSTY
GENIAL	SPRIGHTLY	FALSE	POLISHED
MINOR	STORMY	GAUNT	RELUCTANT
FRESH	FAT	SLIGHT	DULL

Table 1:40
Raw Scores for All Groups

Group 1	Group 2	Group 3	Group 4
$n =$	$n =$	$n =$	$n =$
$\bar{X} =$	$\bar{X} =$	$\bar{X} =$	$\bar{X} =$
$\Sigma X =$	$\Sigma X =$	$\Sigma X =$	$\Sigma X =$
$\Sigma X^2 =$	$\Sigma X^2 =$	$\Sigma X^2 =$	$\Sigma X^2 =$

Summary

This experiment demonstrated that the introduction of newly-learned material between the learning and recall of a task has a deleterious effect upon performance. The effects of material learned just prior to the required learning and recall are less obvious, though sometimes they increase with time.

One of the problems in this experiment is in trying to control the activities of the control groups when they are not learning. If they are simply told to rest they may repeat the learned task over and over again to themselves. For this reason a mechanical task, but one requiring some degree of concentration, has been used.

1   What other ways could be used to occupy the control groups?

2   What might be the effects of using two lists which are very similar, or very dissimilar, in content.

3   What is the relationship between these phenomena and positive and negative transfer of learning?

References

McGEOCH, J. A. Meaningful Relation and Retroactive Inhibition, *American Journal of Psychology*, 43, pp. 579–588, 1931.
SLAMECKA, N. J., & CERASO J. Retroactive and Proactive Inhibition of Verbal Learning, *Psychological Bulletin*, 57, pp. 449–475, 1960.

RE-CODING

Aim

To examine subjects' abilities to recall material, in relation to the degree to which it can be organized into a smaller number of superordinate categories.

Materials

Sufficient viewing frames for all subjects (see details of construction, Appendix 1(b), p. 185, separate sheets with word lists A, B & C for all subjects, pencils and paper for post-test and a stopwatch.

Method

Subjects are randomly assigned to one of three groups. Each group will attempt to memorize each of three word lists as it is exposed through a viewing frame. List A contains words which can be easily 'clustered' into complete categories, e.g. ace, king, queen, jack. List B can also be 'clustered' to some extent, though the categories are not discrete, e.g. England, France, Germany, Russia. Word list C does not offer any clear criterion for establishing categories. To reduce the effects of interference between lists they are allocated as follows:

Group 1	A	B	C
Group 2	B	C	A
Group 3	C	A	B

The experimenter issues the requisite lists and places them in the frames so that the list heading appears through the aperture. He then says: 'Within the viewing frame is a list of words. Every 5 seconds I shall say "change". You are then to slide the sheet upwards so that the next word on the list comes into view. Try to memorize the list, but move on as soon as I tell you to.'

After exposure to the list all groups are required to write down, in any order, as many of the words as they can remember. After a short rest the procedure is repeated twice, using the other word lists. The test sheets are not marked until the experiment is completed.

List A	List B	List C
NORTH	ARM	HAYSTACK
SPRING	MOUNTAIN	REFEREE
MOTHER	BEAN	BEEF
ACE	ENGLAND	TUTOR
ADDITION	DIVAN	GLUE
FATHER	LETTUCE	BULLET
SUMMER	HILL	GARAGE
SUBTRACTION	FRANCE	SOFA
KING	DESK	INK
SOUTH	CARROT	CREEK
MULTIPLICATION	GERMANY	COCOON
QUEEN	TABLE	JUICE
BROTHER	LEG	ARROW
AUTUMN	VALLEY	NOON
EAST	BED	LIBRARY
SISTER	RUSSIA	MONGREL
WINTER	HAND	SHILLING
WEST	CLIFF	FLAG
JACK	POTATO	EYE
DIVISION	HEAD	BASKET

123

Analysis

Subjects are given one mark for each word correctly recalled from the appropriate list. Raw scores are entered on the result sheet.

Table 1:40
Raw Scores for Each List

List A	List B	List C
16	11	9
20	18	18
20	12	10
16	16	15
20	20	10
20	20	17
17	19	15
16	16	16
16	19	16
20	20	13
20	20	13
20	20	13

$n = 12$	$n = 12$	$n = 12$
$\bar{X} = 18.42$	$\bar{X} = 17.58$	$\bar{X} = 13.75$
$\Sigma X = 221$	$\Sigma X = 211$	$\Sigma X = 165$
$\Sigma X^2 = 4113$	$\Sigma X^2 = 3823$	$\Sigma X^2 = 2363$

Below the result sheet is seen the preliminary calculation for an Analysis of Variance (see Appendix 2, Treatment 5, p. 199). The mean recall score for each list ($\bar{X}$) suggests that there is a substantial reduction in recall of List C. Analysis of variance will test between all three lists to determine whether this is statistically significant, or is likely to have occurred by chance. The test is used when there are more than two groups to be tested.

124

Table 1:41
Analysis of Variance

	Sum of squares	d.f.	Mean square	F
Between groups	149	2	74.50	9.84
Within groups	250	33	7.57	
Totals	399	35		

The result of this analysis, $F = 9.84$, is significant at the 0.01 level. That is, there is less than one chance in 100 that such large differences between lists would occur by chance. It can therefore be concluded that when subjects are able to 'cluster' material under category headings they are able to recall greater quantities.

Table 1:42
Raw Scores for Each List

List A	List B	List C

Analysis of Results

Results   (a)   (b)   (c)

Squared scores   (a)   (b)   (c)

1   Total sum of squares   4   Cross-check

2   Sum of squares within groups   5   Analysis of variance

3   Sum of squares between groups

Table 1:43

	Sum of squares	d.f.	Mean square	F
Between groups				
Within groups				
Totals				

Summary

This experiment has demonstrated that, under certain conditions, the usual limits of memory span can be exceeded. This occurs when it is possible for the subject to organize the material into a smaller number of stimulus units by 'clustering' or 're-coding' items. Miller (1956) suggested that the normal span was about seven units, irrespective of their complexity.

The analysis of variance technique does not show the experimenter which groups differed significantly from the others, only that an overall difference occurred. Further tests between pairs of groups would be needed for this purpose, although with the data used here it was fairly obvious that the totally 'unclusterable' group, Group C, was significantly more difficult to recall than the other two.

It is not often that the individual will meet material which lends itself so readily to re-coding as List A, but there are many opportunities for the re-coding of small clusters of items in an idiosyncratic manner.

1   Why were the list sequences altered for the three groups?
2   What sort of interference might one expect between lists?
3   What methods did, or could, the reader devise for coping with List C?

References

BOUSFIELD, W. A. The Occurrence of Clustering in the Recall of Randomly Arranged Associates, *Journal of General Psychology*, 49, pp. 229—240, 1953.

MILLER, G. A. The Magical Number Seven, Plus or Minus Two: Some Limitations on Our Capacity for Processing Information, *Psychological Review*, 63, pp. 81—97, 1956.

TULVING, E. Subjective Organization in Free Recall of 'Unrelated' Words, *Psychological Review*, 69, pp. 344—354, 1962.

MNEMONIC SYSTEMS

Aim

To investigate the efficacy of a mnemonic system in aiding recall of items from specific positions in a word list.

Materials

The experimenter requires word lists A and B. Subjects require two blank sheets of test paper, a copy of system list C, a pencil and a stopwatch.

Method

Subjects will be asked to learn two lists of ten words, matched for frequency of usage. In the first instance they will be given no guidance. Before the second list is learned they will be given a mnemonic system to aid them. The experimenter says: 'I am going to read out a list of words, accompanied by their serial positions. Try to commit the list to memory so that you can recall it in any order I specify.' List A is then read to the subjects with a 10-second interval between items. When the list is completed the subjects are given a blank sheet of paper and asked to write down the words which correspond to the following positions.

(a) 'What was item 9?'   (b)   'What was item 3?' (c)   'What was item 4?'
(d)   ,,   ,,   ,, 8?   (e)   ,,   ,,   ,, 6?   (f)   ,,   ,,   ,, 2?
(g)   ,,   ,,   ,, 1?   (h)   ,,·   ,,   ,, 7?   (i)   ,,   ,,   ,, 5?
(j)   ,,   ,,   ,, 10?

Word list A	Word list B	System list C
1st Turnip	1st Island	One is bun
2nd Baby	2nd Kitchen	Two is shoe
3rd Bad	3rd Nice	Three is tree
4th Anger	4th Devil	Four is door
5th Spanner	5th Compass	Five is hive
6th Tent	6th Family	Six is sticks
7th Birth	7th Bread	Seven is heaven
8th Cushion	8th Spade	Eight is gate
9th Dentist	9th Monkey	Nine is line
10th Mad	10th Bitter	Ten is hen
10 seconds between words	10 seconds between words	

Subjects' responses to the recall test of List A are then scored, and the number out of ten recorded. The time taken to do this is sufficient for them to forget most of that list.

System List C is then given to all subjects and they are asked to memorize it. They may take as long as they wish to do this, but it does not usually take more than 5 minutes. The system list is then removed and the experimenter says: 'Now I am going to read out another list of words which you must memorize so that you can recall it in any order I specify. This time use the interval between words to make a mental link between the word you are trying to memorize and the appropriate word in the system list which signifies its position. For example, if the system list had an item *12 is delve* and you had to remember *12th hard* you might do it by associating the two words in the context *delving into hard ground*. When asked to recall item 12 you could then recall *12 is delve* from the system list; and from that *delve in hard ground*; and thence the word *hard*.' After ensuring that everyone understands the procedure present List B in the same manner as List A. It is then tested in the same way.

Analysis

Raw scores are the individual's number of correctly-recalled words in each test. The scores for all subjects are recorded separately for List A and List B on the results sheet. Comparison of the mean score for each list will give some indication of the possible effects of the mnemonic system, but because individual abilities are likely to be rather diverse the statistical probability of any difference occurring by chance should be tested by means of the t test (Appendix 2, Treatment 4(b), p. 197).

Raw Scores

Table 1:44

List A (no mnemonic)	List B (with mnemonic)
8	10
8	9
8	10
8	7
7	10
7	10
6	9
4	4
7	10
7	9
7	9
5	8
6	7
6	6

$n = 14$ $n = 14$

$\bar{X} = 6.71$ $\bar{X} = 8.43$

$\Sigma X = 94.0$ $\Sigma X = 118.0$

$\Sigma X^2 = 650.0$ $\Sigma X^2 = 1038.0$

Raw Scores

Table 1:45

List A (no mnemonic)	List B (with mnemonic)

$n =$ $n =$

$\bar{X} =$ $\bar{X} =$

$\Sigma X =$ $\Sigma X =$

$\Sigma X^2 =$ $\Sigma X^2 =$

From the analysis by t test a value of 2.21 is obtained for t. This is significant at the 0.05 level, i.e. there is less than one chance in 20 that the difference occurred by chance. It is therefore concluded that the use of the mnemonic system made a significant improvement in the ability of subjects to recall List B.

The results of this experiment are somewhat less predictable than those of previous experiments. Readers may have noticed that there were quite marked differences in the effects of the mnemonic upon the recall rates of individual subjects. This may be because many people automatically adopt strategies for memorizing material. When they are asked to employ some other system this involves deliberately rejecting their own, and making the task much more difficult. Nevertheless, there is evidence that mnemonics are a valuable means of attaching cues to stored material so that it may be more readily recalled.

1   What personalized systems did people in the group use when memorizing List A?
2   Can these systems be classified into different types of mnemonic, and if so, were some types more successful than others?

References

HUNTER, I. M. L. Memory, Chap. 7, Penguin, London, 1964.
NORMAN, D. A. Memory and Attention Chap. 6, John Wiley, New York, 1969.

MEMORY

Man's memory has been a source of wonder to him for many generations. Its importance in the art of rhetoric encouraged the Romans to explore and refine methods for increasing its efficiency, and some of the systems they described are still used today.

Until experimental psychology became systematized at the beginning of this century most studies of memory were concerned with 'capacity' or 'memory span'. This view saw the memory as a unitary process which could be efficient or inefficient. In contemporary social sciences there is still a danger that, in giving hypothetical constructs names, such as 'mind', 'society' or 'memory', they begin to acquire in our imagination all the attributes of objects, such as 'house' or 'muscle'. The muscle analogy is particularly appropriate, for many early writers discussed the value of practice as a means of 'strengthening' mental faculties such as memory, just as one might strengthen the biceps by exercise. William James demonstrated the fallacy of this notion when he heroically memorized 158 lines of poetry before committing the whole of the first volume of *Paradise Lost* to memory. After this latter task — which took him 38 days — he learned another 158 lines of the same poem and found that it took just as long as the first 158 lines. After several replications with remarkably cooperative friends he concluded that memory was not amenable to improvement by exercise.

Experiment 10 investigating 'recall and recognition' offered evidence that the process of memorizing could not be treated as a unitary process. The amount of material remembered was estimated from the amount that the learner could reproduce. Yet if reproduction demanded recall without any cue the score was lower than if subjects had only to recognize items when they saw them again. The differences were of 'output', and if the groups were truly random there was no reason to assume differences of 'input'. McNulty (1965) argued that the output differences revealed the different extents to which the input data had been processed. This hypothesis maintained that recall demanded complete learning, whereas recognition could occur for partially-learned material. An alternative theory, by Hart (1967) suggested that, concurrent with the 'storage' processes were some form of 'labelling' processes which developed cues. These cues enabled the learner to retrieve items from the store as required. In this model items which can be recalled have both processes completed, whereas items which can only be recognized have been stored, but need to be cued by some external source.

Whatever the theoretical interpretation, there is sufficient evidence to conclude that the level of retention is not necessarily indicated by the level of recall. It is intuitively obvious that recognition is easier than recall. Certainly it is that belief which prompts writers to scribble 'friend' and 'freind' in the margin before deciding on the correct spelling (unless they use a mnemonic — which will be discussed later).

Another noticeable difference between memory processes is the difference in the form which reproduced material may take. Whilst the term 'memory store' is in popular use, it is pertinent to ask what is being stored. In everyday life, if we store some fuel we expect to be able to retrieve it as fuel, not as ash, nor as a pack of cards with 'fuel' written on them. Items recalled after a very short time in a memory store, perhaps after 1 or 2 minutes, are very often recalled in their original form. If you wish to make a telephone call and I tell you that the number is 65201, you could probably turn to the telephone and dial it. However, if the telephone was at the other end of the building you might decide to write it down, or to walk along muttering it to yourself, or, if you thought it important enough, you might try to place it in a permanent memory store by some means. The permanent retention would be in a long-term store (LTS), as opposed to the limited duration in the short-term store (STS). The LTS can, as we have seen, take items in their original form; telephone numbers, people's names and poetry must be retained in this form if they are to be of any use. But a great deal of what we store permanently is not reproduced verbatim, although its meaning remains intact. If you were asked to recall a recent conversation with a friend you would probably be able to recount the topic of conversation and the gist of the contributions which you both made, but it is unlikely that you would recall the actual form of the utterances made.

Experiment 11, 'serial recall', gave some indication that more than one process was at work. Two phenomena appeared to have been operative, a 'primacy effect' which stored the early items, and a 'recency effect' which stored the last few items. The effects are thought to be due to processing that takes place in the LTS and STS. The intermediate items were not efficiently stored by either process. Mathematical correction for effects due to long-term memory suggests that the STS can only hold about two or three words at any time, though this is rather speculative (see Craik, 1971).

In a previous paragraph reference was made to repetition as a means of sustaining short-term retention. Atkinson and Shiffrin (1968) have discussed this as one of a number of processes which can occur to items either in STS or in their transition to LTS. For this reason it is not possible to use a time criterion for separating the two memory processes. Nor is it always possible to distinguish the two by the form of reproduction, for reasons which were explained above. Because of the temporal implications of 'long-term' and 'short-term', researchers now tend to use the terms 'secondary' and 'primary' for the processes.

Information-processing models have tended to ascribe forgetting to the use of a wrong 'probe', or cue, with which to extract the stored items from the LTS. This view implies that the content of the store remains intact, though inaccessible. Experiment 12, 'retroactive and proactive inhibition', however, suggested that this may not always be so. The interposing of new items between learning and recall of a task did have an effect; and if the task was repeated after 24 hours an increased effect due to proactive inhibition may have been seen. This suggests that there was some interference between the two lists of items. Inference from this experiment must be restricted because the material had to be stored verbatim. Ausubel and Blake (1958) found no such effects when the stimuli were meaningful prose passages and recall was tested for content, not form. It is presumably difficult for a subject to devise 'probes' which are absolutely distinctive when the stimuli are isolated words or digits. When the stimuli are meaningful, and can be related to a whole network of stored items which the subject already possesses, this may not be the case.

Such explanations are, of course, entirely speculative. The difficulty of assessing what is in the memory store from what is recalled has already been discussed. It is possible that forgetting occurs because of the spontaneous decay of the electrical circuits built up in the brain, or because the wrong 'probe' is being used to try and reach the stored items (Atkinson & Shiffrin, 1971), or because of interference between the required items and other items in the store (Ceraso, 1967).

Even lists of single words can be given meaning if the subject can see some way of forming associations, either between groups of items, or between items and other stored data. Sometimes these associations are quite idiosyncratic and relate to past experience known only to the subject. (On one occasion the author associated 'lawnmower', 'teapot' and 'umbrella' by reference to a family picnic which had recently taken place on the lawn.) At other times material lends itself to obvious groupings, or 'clusters', of items with something in common. Experiment 13, 're-coding', demonstrated that it was possible to subsume relatively large amounts of data under a smaller number of categories, with a substantial improvement in recall. This is known as 'reduction coding' because it reduces the number of stimuli to be dealt with at any one time, though in de-coding again to obtain the original material the overall process will be lengthier. The experiment suggested that the suitability of the material for this type of re-coding was an important variable.

A well-known study by Miller (1956) analysed a number of studies and concluded that memory span could cope with about seven items at any one time, irrespective of the content of the items. Thus, the reduction of the 20 items in Experiment 13 to five groups of four items brought the load well within the capabilities of most people. Because of the mode of presentation of stimuli in this experiment, subjects were unable to survey the data and make a preliminary decision about how they would cluster, as they would normally in a learning situation. Very elaborate coding systems have been devised which allow subjects to handle quite large volumes of data efficiently.

In many cases reduction coding is not possible. In some of them 'elaboration coding' may be more appropriate. Mnemonics are often elaboration codes. They sacrifice brevity in favour of greater coherence and meaning. Memorizing 'Richard Of York Gained Battle In Vain' rather than the initials of the words for the colours of the spectrum is an example of this practice. This is a specific mnemonic, as is the rule 'I before E except after C', though the latter operates in a limited number of situations and might be described as a limited 'mnemonic system' (see Experiment 14).

Mnemonic systems differ from specific mnemonics in that they are generalizable to any combination of letters or figures which are to be memorized. The system used in the experiment was a rather 'loose' one which allowed a good deal of subjective interpretation, and it was limited to lists of ten words. Much more rigorous and sophisticated ones are available, though they demand much more effort to master them (see Hunter, 1964).

References

ATKINSON, R. C., & SHIFFRIN, R. M. Human Memory: A Proposed System and its Control Processes, in SPENCE, K., & SPENCE, J. (Eds) *The Psychology of Learning and Motivation: Advances in Research and Theory* Vol. 2, Academic Press, 1968.

ATKINSON, R. C., & SHIFFRIN, R. M. The Control of Short-Term Memory, *Scientific American*, Aug. 1971, pp. 82–90, 1971.

AUSUBEL, D. P., & BLAKE, E. Proactive Inhibition in the Forgetting of Meaningful School Material, *Journal of Educational Research*, 54, pp. 145–149, 1958.

BADDELEY, A. D. Human Memory, in DODWELL, P. C. (Ed.) *New Horizons in Psychology* Vol. 2, Penguin, London, 1972.

CERASO, J. The Interference Theory of Forgetting, *Scientific American* Oct. 1967, pp. 117–124, (and Reprint No. 509), 1967.

CRAIK, F. I. M. Primary Memory, *British Medical Bulletin*, 27, pp. 323–326, 1971.

HART, J. T. Second-Try Recall, Recognition, and the Memory-Monitoring Process, *Journal of Educational Psychology*, 58, pp. 193–197, 1967.

HOWE, M. J. A. Introduction to Human Memory, Harper & Row, New York, 1970.

HUNTER, I. M. L. Memory, Chap 7, Penguin, London, 1964.

McNULTY, J. A. An Analysis of Recall and Recognition Processes in Verbal Learning, *Journal of Verbal Learning and Verbal Behaviour*, 4, pp. 430–436, 1965.

MILLER, G. A. The Magical Number Seven, Plus or Minus Two: Some Limits on Our Capacity for Processing Information, *Psychological Review*, 63, pp. 81–97, 1956.

NORMAN, D. A. Memory and Attention, J. Wiley, New York, 1969.

MAZE LEARNING

Aim

To measure parts of the learning process used in human maze learning.

Materials

Each pair of participants will need a polystyrene ceiling tile maze, 12 in. (30 cm) square; ten sheets of 14 in. (35 cm) square paper, a watch with a second hand, and a blindfold. Directions for the construction of the maze are given in Appendix 1(*a*), p. 184.

Method

It is essential that the subject to be tested has not seen the maze on which he is to be tested. The experimenter blindfolds the subject and informs him that the object of the experiment is for the subject to find the quickest route from start to finish with the minimum of errors. The experimenter then places the tile maze on top of one of the sheets of paper which he should label Trial 1. He then places the pencil in the hand of the subject and sets the tip of the pencil in the starting groove. Taking care to see that the pencil is always in contact with the paper beneath the tile, the experimenter times the subject's first trial. Subjects are told when they have reached the end of the maze.

The experimenter repeats the procedure until the subject has completed ten trials, taking care to see that each attempt is clearly labelled with its trial number and the time taken. The time taken for each trial should be entered on the recording sheet on p. 138.

Analysis

The experimenter marks the trials by counting one error for each double line that occurs on the route (see Figure 1:9). Occasionally, back-tracking will occur and lines appear in fours and sixes, in each case an additional pair of lines counts as another error on the trial total.

Figure 1:9 A trial sheet showing errors marked

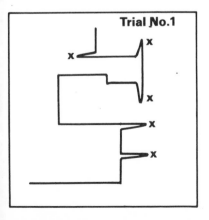

When the experimenter has a set of results for each trial he or she can construct graphs of the type shown on p. 137. These should show the pattern of a subject's learning in terms of time and number of errors.

Summary

The specimen results shown on p. 137 display the type of learning curve usually obtained with this experiment. The errors x trials line on the graph displays an overall decline in the number of errors committed over ten trials. The time x trials line also shows a gradual decline in the amount of time taken to complete the maze route.

This experiment provides an extremely useful introduction to the various theories of learning. It provides students with an experienced example of the learning process with the simpler aspects of learning carefully recorded. Students can usefully consider their results in the following ways. Examine the graph lines for the presence of plateaux. If there are any, try to explain them. Which errors were eliminated first, which later? What was the general shape of the learning curve? Try to explain this. Subjects who attempted the maze should be asked to describe their learning process. Students can discuss their descriptions of their learning in relation to, for example, Hull's Stimulus—Response Theory or Tolman's Cognitive Theory. That is, is maze learning best explained in terms of trial and error learning (Hull) or learning by exploration (Tolman)?

References

HILL, W.F. Learning: A Survey of Psychological Interpretations, Methuen, London, 1963.
HULL, C.L. The Goal Gradient Hypothesis and Maze Learning, Psychology Review 39, pp. 25—43, 1032.
HULL, C. L. Principles of Behavior Appleton-Century, New York, 1943.
SKINNER, B.F. An Operant Analysis of Problem Solving in Problem Solving, Research, Method and Theory, B. Kleinmuntz (Ed.), John Wiley, New York, 1966.
STEVENS, S. S. (Ed.) Handbook of Experimental Psychology, John Wiley, New York, 1951.
TOLMAN, E. C. Purposeful Behavior in Animals and Men, Appleton-Century-Crofts, New York, 1932.
WOODWORTH, R. S., & SCHLOSBERG, H. Experimental Psychology, Methuen, London, 1954.

Figure 1:10 *Maze Learning* (Specimen Results)

Time x Trials Graph

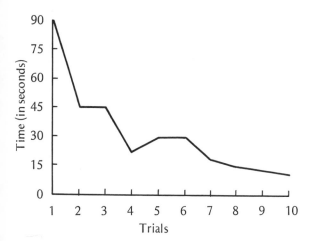

Figure 1:11 *Maze Learning* (Specimen Results)

Errors x Trials Graph

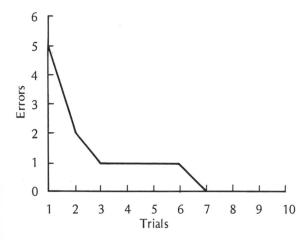

Figure 1:12 Time x Trials

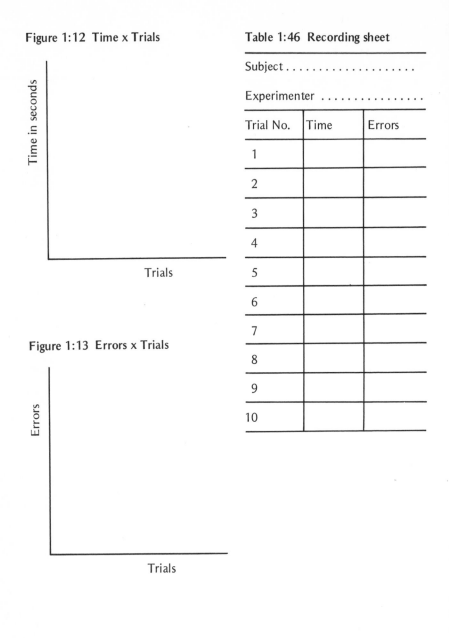

Table 1:46 Recording sheet

Subject . . . .

Experimenter . . . .

Trial No.	Time	Errors
1		
2		
3		
4		
5		
6		
7		
8		
9		
10		

Figure 1:13 Errors x Trials

KNOWLEDGE OF RESULTS

Aim

To show how knowledge of results aids the subject's performance in judging the length of a wooden rod by haptic perception (sense of touch).

Materials

Each pair will need any *one* of the wooden rods accurately cut to lengths of 2, 2½, 3, 3½, 4 in. (approximately 4, 5, 6, 7, 8, 9 cm) — ¼ in. (approximately 5 mm) dowel is suitable, one large sheet of graph paper (1 in. by tenths or a decimal equivalent), and a blindfold.

Method

Pairs of students are randomly divided into Group E (experimental group) and Group C (control group). The instructions for both groups are identical in every respect but one. The common instructions are as follows. A sheet of graph paper is placed in front of the subject who is then blindfolded. The wooden rod is then placed in his hands with the instruction: 'Estimate the length of this rod and draw a line of the same length on the paper in front of you.' Each subject will make 50 attempts to draw a line of the correct length.

The observer moves the paper up after each attempt. The experimental group will operate with this additional instruction. After every attempt to draw a line of the correct length, the observer will check the performance and tell the subject: 'This is correct', or 'That is correct', if the line drawn is within ±¼ in. (approximately 5 mm).

It is very important that only these phrases are used. Feedback will, of course, be variable if some observers say: 'That was almost there' or, 'Oh no! That's a long way out.' The control group subjects will proceed with their 50 attempts without any communication about each attempt. When 50 attempts are complete they will be marked using the same criterion of correct length within ±¼ in. (approximately 5 mm).

Analysis

One mark is given for each correctly-drawn line. Raw scores are entered on the result sheet. The experiment gives us two sets of results — those of the control group which had no knowledge of results, and those from the experimental group which had knowledge of results.

The results shown on p. 140 were obtained when a class of students performed this experiment. Cursory examination suggests that the experimental group has performed at a higher level than the control group. However, we would not expect two groups to produce identical results even under identical conditions. There is a possibility that such differences would occur simply by chance. The *t* test (Appendix 2, Treatment 4(*b*), p. 197) is a test of statistical significance which will tell us if this is so.

Table 1:46

Control Group	Experimental Group
4	2
0	30
16	20
0	38
0	18
3	21
16	26
0	38
12	33
14	2
65	228

$n = 10$ $n = 10$

$\bar{X} = 6.50$ $\bar{X} = 22.80$

$\Sigma X = 65.0$ $\Sigma X = 228.0$

$\Sigma X^2 = 877.0$ $\Sigma X^2 = 6726.0$

From the analysis a value of 7.15 is obtained for t. This is significant at the 0.01 level, i.e. there is less than one chance in a 100 that such differences between groups will have occurred by chance. It is therefore concluded that knowledge of results has produced a significant difference between the two groups.

Table 1:47

Control group   Experimental group

$n =$ $n =$

$\bar{X} =$ $\bar{X} =$

$\Sigma X =$ $\Sigma X =$

$\Sigma X^2 =$ $\Sigma X^2 =$

Summary

This experiment clearly demonstrates the effect of knowledge of results (KR) on performance. An extension of this experiment is to withdraw KR from subjects who have previously had it and observe the deterioration which usually occurs after its removal. Interesting effects can also be observed when the time interval between KR and the next response is controlled and short and long intervals used with two experimental groups.

Students might usefully consider to what degree KR acts as a motivator, and also whether there are any basic similarities between KR used with humans and 'reinforcement' used with animals. Consideration can also be given to the various types of KR and their uses and effectiveness, e.g. verbal and non-verbal KR, concurrent and terminal KR.

References

BAKER, C. H., & YOUNG, P. Feedback During Training and Retention of Motor Skill. Canadian Journal Psychology, 14, pp. 257–264, 1960.

DEESE, J. The Psychology of Learning, McGraw-Hill Book Company Inc., 1958.

HOLDING, D. H. Principles of Training, Pergamon, Oxford, 1965.

LINDGREN H. C., BYRNE, D., & PETRINOVITCH, L. Psychology: an Introduction to Behavioral Science, John Wiley, New York, 1961.

THORNDIKE, E. L. The Law of Effect, American Journal Psychology, 39, pp. 212–222, 1927.

THORNDIKE, E. L. The Fundamentals of Learning, New York Teachers' College, Columbia University, 1932.

LEARNING SET

Aim

To demonstrate the effect of 'set' on the ability to solve anagrams.

Materials

Each pair will need anagram arrays 1 and 2 (see p. 144) each comprising six lists of anagrams, six in each list. The first, third and fifth lists are 'classified', e.g. animals, trees, musical instruments, and the second, fourth and sixth lists are 'unclassified'. A moveable list viewing frame (to construct one see Appendix 1(*b*) p. 185), and a watch with a 'second' hand are required. There is also a complete list of anagram solutions.

Method

The subject is told that he has to try to solve six lists of anagrams, each list containing six different anagrams. Three of the lists are classified, three unclassified. Each anagram will be exposed for 30 seconds but the subject should call out the solution as soon as he is sure he has recognized it. The experimenter's task is as follows. He places the first list in the viewing frame which is then placed in front of the subject. He informs the subject whether the list is classified or unclassified. If the list is classified the subject will be told the list title, e.g. fruit. After alerting the subject, the experimenter exposes the first anagram of the first list, simultaneously noting the time of start, and keeps the anagram exposed for a maximum of 30 seconds. When the subject calls out a solution, the experimenter notes the time. If the solution is given before 30 seconds is up, the experimenter records the recognition time and the response on the recording sheet. If the anagram is not solved in 30 seconds, the experimenter records 'fail' and moves on to the next anagram. This procedure is continued until the end of the list is reached and repeated with the five remaining lists.

Test subject and the experimenter positions can be reversed and the same procedure used with anagram array 2.

Analysis

A useful form of analysis is to compare the number of fails on classified and unclassified lists. This can be done using the arbitrary time limit of 30 seconds to identify failures. A more satisfactory assessment is obtained by taking, as the time limit, the median recognition time of all 36 anagrams. This will give an approximately equal number of fails and passes over the total number of anagrams. Again a simple comparison can be made between the number of fails in the classified and unclassified anagram lists. The procedure for identifying the median is given in Appendix 2, Treatment 2, p. 191.

Summary

The specimen results (Tables 1.48, p. 146, 1.50, p. 148) show clearly that both subjects had a much lower failure rate on the classified anagrams than on the unclassified anagrams. They illustrate the effect of learning set in terms of number of correct solutions and the speed of solution.

Useful discussion of the experiment and its results can be initiated by considering the following questions:

1 Were you aware of any particular obstacles in the way of recognition?
2 Were you aware of any definite procedures in trying to achieve recognition of the word?
3 Did it help you to be told the classification of the list of anagrams? If so, in what ways did this help?

ANAGRAM ARRAY 1

List 1 (animals)	List 2 (unclassified)	List 3 (trees)	List 4 (unclassified)	List 5 (musical instruments)	List 6 (unclass
PEHSE	NUKKS	BHCIR	CLMAE	ANIPO	EBZAR
SHORE	ECEBH	AWNOR	ZAEHL	FETUL	HYLOL
GREIT	GROAN	NPASE	JABON	LELCO	AOVLI
NUKKS	BNIOR	ECEBH	NROEH	GROAN	REVNA
CLMAE	LNMOE	ZAEHL	REPUN	JABON	PLEPA
EBZAR	GIHHT	HYLOL	KENAL	AOVLI	CSTHE

ANAGRAM ARRAY 2

List 1 (birds)	List 2 (unclassified)	List 3 (fruit)	List 4 (unclassified)	List 5 (parts of the body)	List 6 (unclass
TSRKO	SHORE	AEHCP	PEHSE	WTSIR	GRIET
ALGEE	AWNOR	PARGE	BHCIR	TWISA	NPASE
SGOEO	FETUL	ELOVI	ANIPO	OTUMH	LELCO
BNIOR	ALGEE	LNMOE	TSRKO	GIHHT	SGOEO
NROEH	PARGE	REPUN	AEHCP	KENAL	ELOVI
REVNA	TWISA	PLEPA	WTSIR	CSTHE	OTUMH

ANAGRAM ARRAY 1 (SOLUTIONS)

List 1	List 2	List 3	List 4	List 5	List 6
SHEEP	SKUNK	BIRCH	CAMEL	PIANO	ZEBRA
HORSE	BEECH	ROWAN	HAZEL	FLUTE	HOLLY
TIGER	ORGAN	ASPEN	BANJO	CELLO	VIOLA
SKUNK	ROBIN	BEECH	HERON/ RHONE	ORGAN	RAVEN
CAMEL	LEMON/ MELON	HAZEL	PRUNE	BANJO	APPLE
ZEBRA	THIGH	HOLLY	ANKLE	VIOLA	CHEST

ANAGRAM ARRAY 2 (SOLUTIONS)

List 1	List 2	List 3	List 4	List 5	List 6
STORK	HORSE	PEACH	SHEEP	WRIST	TIGER
EAGLE	ROWAN	GRAPE	BIRCH	WAIST	ASPEN
GOOSE	FLUTE	OLIVE	PIANO	MOUTH	CELLO
ROBIN	EAGLE	LEMON/ MELON	STORK	THIGH	GOOSE
HERON	GRAPE	PRUNE	PEACH/ CHEAP	ANKLE	OLIVE
RAVEN	WAIST	APPLE	WRIST	CHEST	MOUTH

Table 1:48
MARKING SHEET (specimen results) using 30-second fails

Classified			Unclassified		
Time	Failures/ Solutions		Time	Failures/ Solutions	
10			15		
8			30		F
9			30		F
10			30		F
30		F	2		
30		F	30		F
10			17		
4			4		
5			30		F
6			30		F
30		F	6		
2			30		F
3			6		
3			4		
3			2		
4			30		F
3			19		
4			8		
		3			8	Total failures

2			7		
5			5		
30		F	3		
1			30		F
1			30		F
2			30		F
2			2		
17			30		F
17			30		F
10			6		
30		F	30		F
2			20		
22			30		F
2			30		F
20			15		
22			30		F
3			13		
2			30		F
		2			10	Total failures

Table 1:49
MARKING SHEET using 30-second fails

Classified   Unclassified

Time   Failures/   Time   Failures/
        Solutions   Solutions

Time	Failures/Solutions		Time	Failures/Solutions	

Total failures

Total failures

148

Table 1:50
MARKING SHEET (specimen results) using median fails

Classified			Unclassified			
Time	Failures/ Solutions		Time	Failures/ Solutions		
10		F	15		F	
8			30		F	
9		F	30		F	
10		F	30		F	
30		F	2			
30		F	30		F	
10		F	17		F	Median 8/9
4			4			
5			30		F	
6			30		F	
30		F	6			
2			30		F	
3			6			
3			4			
3			2			
4			30		F	
3			19		F	
4			8			
		7			11	Total failures

2			7			
5			5			
30		F	3			
1			30		F	
1			30		F	
2			30		F	
2			2			
17		F	30		F	Median 16
17		F	30		F	
10			6			
30		F	30		F	
2			20		F	
22		F	30		F	
2		F	30		F	
20			15			
22		F	30		F	
3			13			
2			30		F	
		7			11	Total failures

Table 1:51
MARKING SHEET using median fails

Classified			Unclassified			
Time	Failures/ Solutions		Time	Failures/ Solutions		
						Median
						Total failures

						Median
						Total failures

References

ANDERSON, B., & JOHNSON, W. Two Kinds of Set in Problem Solving, *Psychological Reports,* **19**, pp. 851—858, 1966.
BARTLETT, F. C. Remembering, Cambridge University Press, 1932.
HUNTER, I. M. L. The Influence of Mental Set on Problem Solving, *British Journal Psychology,* 47, pp. 63—64, 1956.
HUNTER, I. M. L. The Solving of Five-Letter Anagram Problems, *British Journal Psychology,* 50, pp. 193—206, 1959.
JOHNSON, D. M. The Psychology of Thought and Judgement, Harper & Row, New York, (Contains an extended discussion of 'set' Chap. 6), 1955.
LUCHINS, A. S. Classroom Experiments on Mental Set, *American Journal Psychology,* 59, pp. 295—298, 1946.

CONCEPT FORMATION IN CHILDREN

Introduction

This experiment is somewhat different from the others in this manual. It provides a means of examining the concepts made by a sample of children, or the test results from one child can be compared with the results presented here. Concepts are the results of thought processes which group objects or ideas according to some characteristics which they have in common. 'Colour' and 'size' are simple criteria for the formation of concepts; 'function' and 'origin' are rather more sophisticated, and may be considered representative of later stages of intellectual development.

The design is adapted from that used by Annett (1959).

Aim

The experiment investigates the formation and use of four common class concepts by primary school children (aged from 5 to 11 years).

Materials

The apparatus consists of 16 white cards of equal size (see Figures 1:14 and 1:15), about 3 x 3 in. On each of these is a simple black line drawing depicting one of the following:

horse	flower	car	boat
fish	mushroom	aeroplane	locomotive
bird	apple	television set	chair
butterfly	tree	desk	clock

To ensure success it is essential that the cards be constructed with great care. The drawings should show no colour or background and no variables should exist in the shapes of the cards. For example, all drawings should be of similar size, lines should all be of the same density and thickness and, if the cards are not square but rectangular, they must all be used the same way round.

Method

Children are tested individually. The experimenter records the age of the subject, then lays out the cards in a random order which has been determined beforehand. This control is necessary if several experimenters are working on the same project.

In the results shown on p. 156—158 the cards were arranged in two rows of eight. It has since been shown that the mode of display does influence results (Brown, Shaw and Taylor, 1969). The experimenter then says: 'Some of these cards belong together. Put together those which belong.' If the subject does not seem to understand the instructions they should be repeated, but no further help should be given.

The content of each group made by the subject is carefully recorded. When this is finished the experimenter points to each group in turn and says: 'Why do these belong together?' The explanations for each group are recorded in full.

152

Figure 1:14

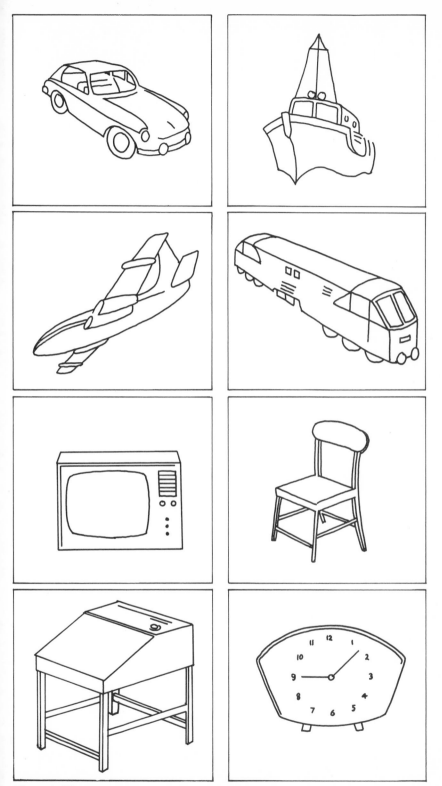

Figure 1:15

It must be emphasized that experimental recording requires great attention to detail, unfinished sentences, alterations etc. must all be included. A tape-recorder is a useful, though not an essential, aid in this task.

Analysis

The data are to be analysed in two ways. Firstly by recording the total number of groups used, and secondly by examining the reason for these groupings as shown by the type of explanation used.

1 The number of groups made by the subject is recorded. Isolated cards count as a group. A serial group of 16 cards is also counted as a group. If the groupings are so small that the total number of groups exceeds ten this is recorded as zero groups.

2 Each explanation is then classified by the experimenter, according to the criteria given on p. 155. Experimenters should ideally exchange data and reclassify to ensure that explanations have been properly interpreted.

From this analysis the experimenter can determine which criterion was most frequently used by the subject. If two classes of explanation were equally used ½ is scored in each category.

When the subject has given more than one explanation each must be accepted and classified separately, unless it is clear that one was withdrawn.

The following analysis is of the responses made by 200 junior schoolchildren. Figure 1:16 indicates the percentage of responses in each age group employing zero to ten classifications. Note the predominance of eight pairs of cards in the earlier years. Figure 1:17 is an enlarged treatment of the central portion of Figure 1:16. The gradual decrease of eight pairs until it is superseded by four groups of four can be clearly seen. Figure 1:18 shows the percentage of each age group with which each type of explanation predominated. (The five criteria have not been subdivided in this analysis.)

The reader may wish to investigate these results in greater depth. Analysis by sex as well as by age could be attempted.

Criteria for Explaining Groupings

1 No explanation — 'Don't know', 'They just go together', 'They belong', etc.

2 Enumeration — give facts about each object, but different facts about each one.

> (a) Describes one of the objects, e.g. tree, cow and flower explained by 'the tree is in the field'.
> (b) Naming — 'This is a cow', 'This is a bird', etc.
> (c) Place — 'The cow is on the farm and the fish is in the sea'.

3 Contiguity — objects related by direct, concrete interaction.

> (a) Place — 'The apple grows on the tree'.
> (b) Time — 'You can see by the clock when it's time for television'.
> (c) Animal activity — 'Butterflies settle on flowers'.

(*d*) Human activity – 'You sit on the chair to watch television'.
(*e*) Serial contiguities – a large number of objects related in a series of contiguities.

4 Similarities – characteristic common to the objects.

(*a*) Place – 'The fish and the ship are in/on the sea'.
(*b*) Activity – 'They fly', 'They grow', 'They run along'.
(*c*) Human activity – 'People ride in them', 'You sit on them'.
(*d*) Structure – 'All wooden', 'All have wheels', 'All have stalks'.

5 Class name – class name given, even if not entirely appropriate ('Creatures', 'Machines', 'Pets', etc.).

Figure 1:16
Concept formation in children

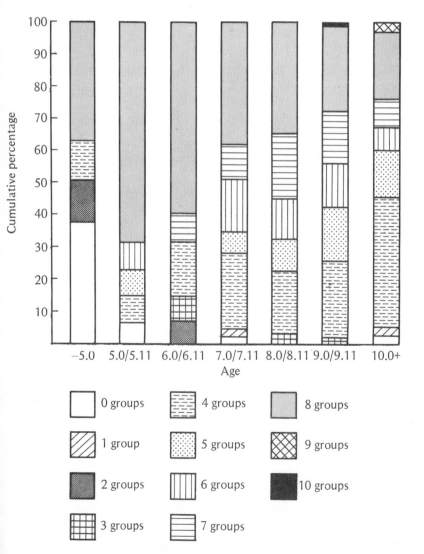

Figure 1:17
Concept formation in children,

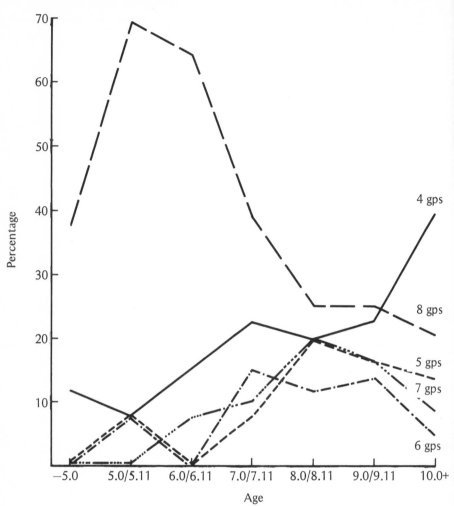

Figure 1:18
Concept formation in children

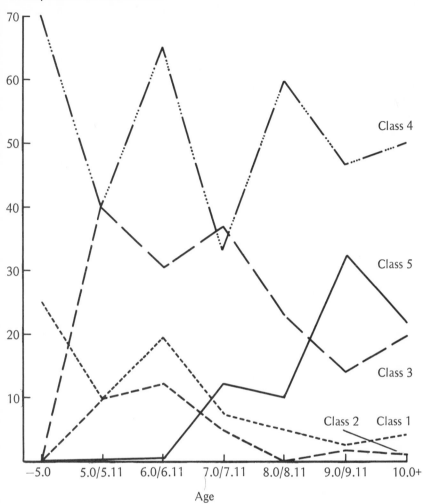

Summary

The development of class concepts plays an important role in the child's growing comprehension of the adult world. It is that part of the child's intellectual development which attempts to simplify the perception of the environment by classifying objects or ideas according to particularly common characteristics. This experiment reveals the slow evolution of four common class concepts in young children. There is a general trend towards the use of 'sophisticated' class concepts as age increases. However, within each age-group students will find a wide range of individual differences. The possible reasons for these differences will provide an interesting basis for discussion. It may result, for example, from the simple inability of the youngest children to fully comprehend the verbal instructions or, as Brown *et al.*, (1969) suggest, that the layout of card presentation is a significant factor. Perhaps the most important factor to emerge is the steadily increasing use of class names by children as criteria for explanation. This indicates how dangerous it can be for adults to assume that children will understand and be able to use adult class concepts.

References

ANNETT, M. The Classification of Instances of Four Common Class Concepts, *British Journal Educational Psychology*, 29, pp. 223–236, 1959.
BROWN, G., SHAW, M. and TAYLOR, S. An Experiment to Examine the Use of Four Common Class Concepts by Primary Schoolchildren, *Papers in Education*, Journal of Anstey College of P.E. No. 1, 1969.
STONES, E. An Introduction to Educational Psychology, Methuen, London, 1966.
STONES, E., and HESLOP, J. R. The Formation and Extension of Class Concepts in Primary Schoolchildren, *British Journal Educational Psychology*, 38, pp. 261–271, 1968.

LEARNING BEHAVIOUR

The systematic interpretation of learning has an important place in the study of psychology, and in the application of psychology to education. As with so many issues in psychology, no one theory has provided all the answers to questions concerning the mechanics of learning. Indeed, all the theories put together do not provide us with all the answers. The student often, therefore, has initially to adopt a pragmatic approach — choosing, from his own learning experience, those points which he feels relate to his own learning mechanisms. It is usually from this anecdotal base that a study of learning begins.

Although psychological learning theory has been introduced with some reserve and caution, there are many positive reasons for giving it attention. Learning theories consist, mainly, of statements purporting to be experimentally verifiable hypotheses, but they differ significantly in the conceptual models which they use e.g. concepts of stimulus response, insight learning, learning hierarchies, etc. (see Child, 1973). The experiments in this section provided an opportunity for tutors and students to make some initial exploratory studies of their own learning behaviour and relate these to the literature on learning theory.

Experiment 15, 'maze learning', was concerned with two simple manifestations of the process of learning the correct route through the maze, i.e. time taken, and number of errors made. This gave us two simple measures of learning effectiveness. The more significant factors for the student of learning theory were the processes underlying the overall decline in time and errors. With groups of students one invariably finds that all improve performance, but in discussion, it becomes evident that the processes used to achieve this often vary from one person to another.

The method of learning varies. Some use simple internalized route instructions learned by trial and error, e.g. first left, second right, etc. Others have a mental map which can vary from the simple map of the correct route to the sophisticated map which includes all the blind alleys. Still others may use the 'safe surface' method, i.e. choosing the side of the channel which produces the least number of errors. There are also some who, after two or three trials, can produce a simple flowing movement which might almost suggest 'muscle memory'. In addition to the wide range of methods manifested by a group of students, it will probably be found that even an individual student has used various combinations of these methods within his ten trials. Experiment 15 provides tutors and students with a common and relatively controlled learning situation as the basis for a full discussion of some of the concepts used in learning theory.

Experiment 16, 'knowledge of results', demonstrates the way in which knowledge of results can influence one's subsequent performance. Knowledge of results is, perhaps, one of the most general features of all learning situations. Its role in changing and controlling behaviour has been a focus of research for many years (see Annett 1969). The experiment illustrates a learning phenomenon which leads us into the field of behaviourist learning theory. Thorndike's Law of Effect predicts that, in a novel situation, any response which is successful is likely to be 'stamped in'. In the learning situation correct responses can only be acquired if the learner knows that they are correct. This process is often called 'feedback', i.e. a knowledge of the previous attempt is 'fed back' to modify the next. In addition, the concept of feedback introduces the student to the servomechanistic model of learning. This model likens the human organism to the various electrical or mechanical machines which can initiate new operations in response to change.

Experiment 17, 'learning set', demonstrated the effect that a preparatory adjustment or readiness for a particular activity can have on learning performance. Learning and performance are obviously aided when attention is focused on the essential and relevant features of a problem. Studies of human learning have revealed that an ability to learn how to solve problems of a given kind can be developed with sufficient practice on a task of a similar nature. The experiment involves a standard task, i.e. the solution of anagrams. Success, in terms of speed of solution of certain groups of anagrams, is seen to be accelerated by the distinctiveness of the learning set used, i.e. that the anagrams are categorized. Much of the process of education could be regarded as the formation of learning sets. Much of adult problem-solving ability is dependent upon learning sets derived from prior experience in learning.

Experiment 18, 'concept formation in children', was somewhat different from the others in this section in that as well as being a simple fieldwork exercise it also provided a means of examining the concepts formed by a sample of children; or, alternatively, enabled the test results from one child to be compared with the results illustrated in the experiment. The experiment also brought to light the possibility that the child may interpret his environment in ways which are no longer familiar to the adult. Such a thesis is central to the work of Piaget (see Phillips, 1969).

Concepts are the products of thought processes which group objects or ideas according to characteristics which they have in common. 'Colour' and 'size' are simple criteria for the formation of concepts; 'function' and 'origin' are rather more sophisticated, and they may be considered representative of later stages of intellectual development. The experiment gives a useful introduction to the developmental aspects of learning behaviour.

References

ANNETT, J. Feedback and Human Behaviour, Penguin, London, 1969.
BORGER, R., & SEABORNE, E. M. The Psychology of Learning, Pelican, London, 1966.
CHILD, D. Psychology and the Teacher, Holt, Rinehart and Winston, London, 1973.
HILL, W. F. Learning: A Survey of Psychological Interpretations. Methuen, London, 1964.
PHILLIPS, J. L. The Origins of Intellect: Piaget's Theory, Freeman, 1969.

NEED FOR ACHIEVEMENT

Aim

To examine the association between students' need for achievement and their intended career paths.

Method

Subjects complete:

1 The appropriate (male or female) form of the Mehrabian need for achievement scale, a 26-item instrument anglicized and validated for use with British students by Cohen, Reid and Boothroyd (1973).

2 A career aspiration instrument in the form of a grid representing various areas of a chosen occupational field.

In the example below the career aspiration grid has been designed for use with students who will enter the field of education. The grid has three career paths — schools, educational administration, and higher education. Each of the career paths has been illustrated by what are generally held to be initial, intermediate and top-level career positions arrayed along a 9-interval scale. For example, initial posts (scale position 1) for each of the three career paths are given as assistant teacher, administrative assistant, and assistant lecturer, respectively. Intermediate posts (scale position 5) are depicted as head of department, adviser/organizer, and university lecturer or senior lecturer in a college of education. Similarly top-level posts (scale position 9) are represented by head teacher, director of education, professor or principal. Subjects circle the scale number they aspire to on the appropriate career path at 25, 35, and 45 years of age.

Experimenters will devise their own grids (appropriate to their subject populations) illustrating the career paths by initial, intermediate, and top-level posts.

Male need for achievement scale

The following questionnaire of personal attitudes consists of a number of items worded as: 'I'd rather do (A) than (B)', such as, 'I'd rather go swimming than bowling'. You are to indicate the extent of your agreement with each item using the scale below. Please note that if you give strong agreement to the statement: 'I'd rather do (A) than (B)', this indicates that you prefer (A) much more than (B). If you give strong disagreement to that statement, this indicates that you prefer (B) much more than (A).

Indicate, for each item, the extent of your agreement or disagreement with that item by entering the appropriate numeral (+4 to −4) in the space provided by each item.

+4 = Very strong agreement
+3 = Strong agreement
+2 = Moderate agreement
+1 = Slight agreement
 0 = Neither agreement nor disagreement
−1 = Slight disagreement
−2 = Moderate disagreement
−3 = Strong disagreement
−4 = Very strong disagreement

1   I worry more about getting a bad mark than I think about getting a good mark.   ....

2   I would rather work on a task where I alone am responsible for the final product than one in which many people contribute to the final product.   ....

3   I more often attempt difficult tasks that I am not sure I can do than easier tasks I believe I can do.   ....

4   I would rather do something at which I feel confident and relaxed than something which is challenging and difficult.   ....

5   If I am not good at something I would rather keep struggling to master it than move on to something I may be good at.   ....

6   I would rather have a job in which my role is clearly defined by others and my rewards could be higher than average, than a job in which my role is to be defined by me and my rewards are average.   ....

7   I would prefer a well-written informative book to a good film.   ....

8   I would prefer a job which is important, difficult, and involves a 50 per cent chance of failure to a job which is somewhat important but not difficult.   ....

9   I would rather learn fun games that most people know than learn unusual skill games which only a few people would know.   ....

10   It is very important for me to do my work as well as I can even if it means not getting along well with my co-workers.   ....

11   For me, the pain of getting turned down after a job interview is greater than the pleasure of getting hired.   ....

12   If I am going to play cards I would rather play a fun game than a difficult thought game.   ....

13   I prefer competitive situations in which I have superior ability to those in which everyone involved is about equal in ability.   ....

14   I think more of the future than of the present and past.   ....

15   I am more unhappy about doing something badly than I am happy about doing something well.   ....

16   In my spare time I would rather learn a game to develop skill than for recreation.   ....

17   I would rather run my own business and face a 50 per cent chance of bankruptcy than work for another firm.   ....

18   I would rather take a job in which the starting salary is £1,500 and could stay that way for some time than a job in which the starting salary is £1,000 and there is a guarantee that within five years I will be earning more than £1,500.   ....

19   I would rather play in a team game than compete with just one other person.   ....

20   The thing that is most important for me about learning to play the guitar is being able to play a musical instrument very well, rather than learning it to have a better time with my friends.   ....

21   I prefer multiple-choice questions on exams to essay questions.   ....

22   I would rather work on commission which is somewhat risky but where I would have the possibility of making more than working on a fixed salary.   ....

23   I think that I hate losing more than I love winning.   ....

24   I would rather wait 1 or 2 years and have my parents buy me one great gift than have them buy me several average gifts over the same period of time.   ....

25   If I were able to return to one of two uncompleted tasks, I would rather return to the difficult than the easy one.   ....

26   I think more about my past accomplishments than about my future goals.   ....

Female need for achievement scale

The following questionnaire of personal attitudes consists of a number of items worded as: 'I'd rather do (A) than (B)' such as: 'I'd rather go swimming than go bowling'. You are to indicate the extent of your agreement with each item using the scale below. Please note that if you give strong agreement to the statement: 'I'd rather do (A) than (B)', this indicates that you prefer (A) much more than (B). If you give strong disagreement to that statement, this indicates that you prefer (B) much more than (A).

Indicate, for each item, the extent of your agreement or disagreement with that item by entering the appropriate numeral (+4 to —4) in the space provided by each item.

+4 = Very strong agreement
+3 = Strong agreement
+2 = Moderate agreement
+1 = Slight agreement
 0 = Neither agreement nor disagreement
—1 = Slight disagreement
—2 = Moderate disagreement
—3 = Strong disagreement
—4 = Very strong disagreement

1   I think more about getting a good mark than I worry about getting a bad mark. ....

2   I more often attempt difficult tasks that I am not sure I can do than easier tasks I believe I can do. ....

3   I would rather do something at which I feel confident and relaxed than something which is challenging and difficult. ....

4   If I am not good at something I would rather keep struggling to master it than move on to something I may be good at. ....

5   I would rather have a job in which my role is clearly defined by others and my rewards could be higher than average, than a job in which my role is to be defined by me and my rewards are average. ....

6   My strongest feelings are aroused more by fear of failure than by hope of success. ....

7   I would prefer a well-written informative book to a good film. ....

8   I would prefer a job which is important, difficult, and involves a 50 per cent chance of failure to a job which is somewhat important but not difficult. ....

9   I would rather learn fun games that most people know than learn unusual skill games which only a few people would know. ....

10   It is very important for me to do my work as well as I can even if it means not getting along well with my co-workers. ....

11   For me, the pain of getting turned down after a job interview is greater than the pleasure of getting hired. ....

12   If I am going to play cards I would rather play a fun game than a difficult game. ....

13   I prefer competitive situations in which I have superior ability to those in which everyone involved is about equal in ability. ....

14 I think more of the future than of the present and past. ....

15 I am more unhappy about doing something badly than I am happy about doing something well. ....

16 I worry more about whether people will praise my work than I do about whether they will criticize it. ....

17 If I had to spend the money myself I would rather have an exceptional meal out than spend less and prepare an exceptional meal at home. ....

18 I would rather do a paper on my own than take a test. ....

19 I would rather share in the decision-making process of a group than take total responsibility for directing the group's activities. ....

20 I would rather try to make new and interesting meals that may turn out badly than make more familiar meals that frequently turn out well. ....

21 I would rather do something I enjoy than something that I think is worth while but not much fun. ....

22 I would rather try to get two or three things done quickly than spend all my time working on one project. ....

23 If I am ill and must stay at home, I use the time to relax and recuperate rather than try to read or work. ....

24 If I were rooming with a number of girls and we decided to have a party, I would rather organize the party myself than have one of the others organize it. ....

25 I would rather cook for a couple of gourmet eaters than for a couple who simply have huge appetites. ....

26 I would rather be allowed to help organize social service projects by women's groups than be allowed to work on the projects after they have been organized. ....

Career Aspiration Grid

We would like you to use this questionnaire to plot your intended career, indicating by encircling three numbers, the positions you hope to reach at 25, 35, and 45 years of age.

The scales below represent the range of professional positions commonly found in schools, educational administration, and higher education. They consist of nine points numbered 1 to 9 and you will see that examples are given as guides of high, intermediate, and low positions in each of the three fields. You are asked to indicate the level you hope to reach by the time you are 25 by circling the appropriate number (1 to 9) in the appropriate column, (school, educational administration, or higher education) and writing 25 next to it.

Similarly, you are asked to indicate the level and the field in which you expect to be working at 35. Do the same for your expectations at 45 years of age. It may be that your three circles all occur in one column or that they are in two or three columns. This, of course, is precisely what we wish to find out, namely, your intended career pattern as far as you are able to judge at the moment.

School	Educational administration	Higher education
	Top level	
9 Head teacher	9 Director of education	9 University professor
8	8	8
7	7	7
6	6	6
	Intermediate level	
5 Head of department .	5 Adviser, organizer in a local education authority	5 Senior lecturer in a college of education or lecturer in university
4	4	4
3	3	3
2	2	2
	Low level	
1 Assistant teacher	1 Administrative assistant	1 Assistant lecturer in college or research assistant in university

Scoring the need for achievement scale.

To compute a total score, first change the sign of the subject's response on all negative items. Then obtain an algebraic sum of the 26 scores.

Male		Female	
Item	Item	Item	Item
1–	14+	1+	14+
2+	15–	2+	15–
3+	16+	3–	16+
4–	17+	4+	17–
5+	18–	5–	18+
6–	19–	6–	19–
7+	20+	7+	20+
8+	21–	8+	21–
9–	22+	9–	22–
10+	23–	10+	23–
11–	24+	11–	24+
12–	25+	12–	25+
13–	26–	13–	26+

Analysis

In a recent study (Cohen, Reid and Boothroyd, 1973) male and female student teachers completed the Mehrabian 'need for achievement' scale and indicated their intended career paths on the career aspiration instrument at 25, 35 and 45 years of age. It was found that, whereas nearly all students saw their early careers in schools, there was evidence of differentiation in career paths by 45 years of age. In Table 1:52 below, the mean need for achievement scores of students aspiring to *school-based* careers are compared with the scores of those aspiring to *higher education* positions at 45 years of age. The hypothesis was that high need for achievement would be associated with a desire to move out of positions of less-prestige (schools) and into posts of greater prestige (in higher education). Table 1:52 shows that the hypothesis was supported in both the male and female group analyses.

Table 1:52

Mean need for achievement scores of male and female students aspiring to school and higher education career posts

Career	Male			Female		
	$\bar{x}$	s.d.	n	$\bar{x}$	s.d.	n
Schools	7.59	16.13	80	–2.09	16.40	194
Higher education	12.62	16.23	43	9.06	19.33	32

$t = 1.66 \quad p < 0.05$ (one-tailed test) $\quad t = 3.09 \quad p < 0.01$ (one-tailed test)

Note that because *direction* was predicted in respect of the scores on need for achievement of two differing groups a one-tailed *t* test was appropriate to the analysis (see Appendix 2, Treatment 4(*a*) p. 196 for *t* test; and glossary (p. 236) for one-tailed analysis). In the same study (Cohen, Reid, Boothroyd, 1973) there was the rather unusual finding that students with *very low* need for achievement nevertheless held unrealistically high career aspirations at 45 years of age. The researchers identified very low and very high need for achievement by grouping together those subjects whose need for achievement scores fell ± one standard deviation from the mean (see Appendix 2, Treatment 3, p. 194 for standard deviation and glossary (p. 235) for normal distribution). The analysis of the career aspirations of extreme need for achievement groups is given in Table 1:53 below:

Table 1:53

Career aspirations at 45 years of age of extreme need for achievement groups

(*n* = 58 male students)

Career	High need	Low need
Schools	15	10
Higher education	10	23

$x^2 = 3.97$ d.f. = 1, $p < 0.05$ (with Yates' correction)

A measure of association suitable for 2 x 2 tables is Phi (ϕ) (see Appendix 2, Treatment 10, p. 211). In respect of Table 1:53 phi provides us with a statistic by which to describe the strength of the relationship between career choice and need for achievement. Phi would be useful should, for example, we wish to compare the strength of that relationship at say, 25, 35 and 45 years of age. The significance of phi is taken directly from the chi-square value. In Table 1:53 above:

$$\phi(\text{phi}) = \sqrt{\frac{x^2}{N}} = \sqrt{\frac{3.97}{58}} = 0.26$$

Analysis

1   Compute mean scores and standard deviations on need for achievement for males and females separately.

2   Compute mean scores and standard deviations for 'A'-level performance for males and females separately (see Experiment 7, Treatments 1 and 3, pp. 190 and 194 for detailed instructions).

3   Examine the degree of association between need for achievement and 'A'-level performance in the male and female groups. Dichotomize the male group at the mean score on 'A'-level performance to give high and low groups. Using the mean score on need for achievement from item 1 above cast the data in a 2 x 2 table as in Table 1:54 below:

Table 1:54

Need for achievement

Males

'A'-level performance		High	Low	Totals
	High			
	Low			

$$\chi^2 = \underline{\hspace{3cm}} \qquad p = \underline{\hspace{3cm}}$$

$$\phi = \sqrt{\frac{\chi^2}{N}} = \underline{\hspace{3cm}}$$

4   Repeat for the female group:

Table 1:55

Need for achievement

Females

'A'-level performance		High	Low	Totals
	High			
	Low			

$$\chi^2 = \underline{\hspace{3cm}} \qquad p = \underline{\hspace{3cm}}$$

$$\phi = \sqrt{\frac{\chi^2}{N}} = \underline{\hspace{3cm}}$$

5   Interpret the differences in the degree of association between 'A'-level performance and need for achievement in male and female groups below.

_____

_____

_____

_____

_____

6 Cast the career aspiration grid into the form below (males and females separately at first).

Table 1:56

Males

		Lower status path (school)		Higher status path (educational admin. + higher education)	
Top level	(9)		1		2
	(8)				
	(7)				
Inter-mediate levels.	(6)		3		4
	(5)				
	(4)				
Low level	(3)		5		6
	(2)				
	(1)				

Sort male career aspirations at 45 years of age (or 25, 35) into the six cells of the reformed Career Aspiration Grid above. Compute the mean score and standard deviation on need for achievement for subjects assigned to each of the six cells. Use the t test to examine differences in need for achievement between various cells (see Appendix 2, Treatment 4, p. 196).

Note

It may be necessary to combine cells in these analyses. For example, in the lower status path (schools) at 45 years of age, numbers in the cells may require 'intermediate' and 'low' cells to be combined. Similarly, in the lower status path (schools) and the higher status path (educational admin. + higher education) at 35 years of age, numbers in the cells may require 'top level' and 'intermediate level' cells to be combined.

7   On the male career aspiration grid (45 years of age) compare:

Higher status path (top level) cell 2

and lower status path (low level) cell 5

$t =$ _____ $p =$ _____

Select other cell combinations for comparison, e.g. 1–2; 3–4; 5–6; 1–5; 2–6, etc. Is it possible to discern a trend in the relationship between need for achievement and the career aspirations of the subjects?

_____

_____

_____

8   Repeat for female group.

9   If numbers are small combine male and female groups into one table as above. Calculate the mean score and standard deviation on need for achievement for each cell in this combined sample. Repeat t tests between selected groups, e.g.:

Higher status path (top level) cell   2   2

and lower status path (low level) cell 5

$t =$ _____ $p =$ _____

Select other cell combinations for comparison, e.g. 1–2; 3–4; 5–6; 1–5; 2–6, etc. Again, is it possible to discern a trend in the relationship between need for achievement and the career aspirations of the subjects?

_____

_____

_____

_____

10   Separate out males (very low need for achievement) and males (very high need for achievement) by taking those whose scores lie ± one standard deviation from the mean (see Appendix 2, Treatment 3, p. 194 for standard deviation and glossary (p. 235) for normal distribution). Repeat the procedure for the female group. What is the relationship between very low need for achievement and career aspirations?

172

Table 1:57

Males (at 45 years of age) or 35, 25 as appropriate

Group	Lower status career — schools	Higher status career — admin. + higher educ.
Low need for achievement		
High need for achievement		

$$\chi^2 = \underline{\hspace{3cm}} \qquad p = \underline{\hspace{3cm}}$$

$$\phi = \sqrt{\frac{\chi^2}{N}} = \underline{\hspace{4cm}}$$

Females (at 45 years of age) or 35, 25 as appropriate

Group	Lower status career — schools	Higher status career — admin. + higher educ.
Low need for achievement		
High need for achievement		

$$\chi^2 = \underline{\hspace{3cm}} \qquad p = \underline{\hspace{3cm}}$$

$$\phi = \sqrt{\frac{\chi^2}{N}} = \underline{\hspace{4cm}}$$

Further Applications

Use the self-identity questionnaire (see Experiment 7, p. 69) in conjunction with the need for achievement scale. Examine the relationship between various self-identities in male and female groups and need for achievement.

References

COHEN, L., REID, I., and BOOTHROYD, K. Validation of the Mehrabian Need for Achievement Scale with College of Education Students, *British Journal of Educational Psychology*, 43, 3, 1973.

REID, I., and COHEN, L. Achievement Orientation, Intellectual Achievement Responsibility, and Choice Between Degree and Certificate Courses in Colleges of Education, *British Journal of Educational Psychology*, 43, 1, 1973.

REID, I., and COHEN, L. Male and Female Achievement Orientation and Intellectual Responsibility: A British Validation Study. *Educational and Psychological Measurement*, 34, pp. 379-382, 1974.

DIFFERENCES IN TASTE PERCEPTION

Aim

To investigate the frequency of phenyl thiocarbamide (PTC) tasters in the class.

Materials

Obtain a solution of PTC from a chemist or a biology laboratory. It should be made by dissolving 0.13 g of PTC in a little boiling water and making up to 100 ml. Cut some absorbent paper into pieces of approximately 2 cm by 3 cm and soak them in the solution. Dry them and store in an envelope. (They will keep for about a month.)

Note: PTC is dangerous. Do not exceed the concentration recommended.

Method

Each subject is given one piece of paper from the envelope. The following instructions are given: 'Take the piece of paper and place it on your tongue. Count silently to twenty, remove the paper, and dispose of it. Put a tick in the appropriate square on p. 256 to indicate whether you tasted nothing, a slight taste, or a strong taste. *Do not repeat the tasting.*

Analysis

The number of subjects responding in each category is then recorded.

Frequency of Tasters and Non-Tasters

No taste	Slight taste	Strong taste
8	6	9

From the above table it is clear that there is no agreement in the group as to whether the paper has any taste at all. The ability to taste PTC is dependent upon a specific dominant gene, and only a specific proportion of the population has this gene.

Frequency of Tasters and Non-Tasters

No taste	Slight taste	Strong taste

Summary

For the purposes of this experiment it is sufficient to demonstrate that there are differences in certain perceptual abilities between individuals. It is unlikely that this one is of much significance for the social sciences, but it is wise to remember that there may be inter-subject discrepancies at a fundamental level. Theoretically, the population is divided into those who can, and those who cannot, taste PTC. It is probable that subjects who think they detect a slight taste are non-tasters responding to the taste of the paper. Here, this is unimportant, but for biologists wishing to calculate frequencies it is customary to add the 'no taste' and 'slight taste' cells together.

Reference

NUFFIELD FOUNDATION The Perpetuation of Life – Nuffield Biology Teachers' Guide V, Longmans/Penguin, London, 1967.

RESPONSE LATENCIES

Aim

To examine the relationship between a subject's speed of response (response latency) to a word association test and the subsequent recall of the stimulus words.

Materials

Each pair will need two word lists (see pp. 176–177) and a stopwatch which will measure fractions of a second.

Method

The subject is told that he is going to be given a word association test. The experimenter then says: 'I shall say a word, and I want you to respond with the first word that comes into your head.' The experimenter should take care not to indicate that recall will be required later, and should make a brief pause between words so that the subject does not become anxious. The time taken for each response is carefully recorded (the time for a response is measured from the end sound of the stimulus word to the end sound of the response). The response and the response time are both recorded on the word association test sheets.

After the test, the experimenter can silently read through the results – so that a period of at least 5 minutes elapses before anything further is required of the subject. During this time the subject must not see the test sheets. Thereafter, the subject is required to write down from memory, on a separate sheet of paper, as many of the stimulus words he can remember, in any order.

Analysis

On the word association test sheets are four columns labelled S, L, R and F. They are used as follows: S and L stand for short and long response latency. A response given within 1.5 seconds or less is considered short (S) response latency, whereas a response given in excess of 1.5 seconds is long (L) response latency. The approximate mean response latency as given by Woodworth and Schlosberg (1966) is 1.5 seconds which is derived from the results of a number of other experiments in this field. All 48 responses should be designated as either S or L response latencies on the test sheets. Columns R and F are used to record stimulus words recalled (R) or forgotten (F).

Table 1:59

Stimulus	Response	Time	S	L	R	F
Cook						
Red						
Smooth						
Below						
Baby						
Grope						
Car						
Jewel						
Alone						
Paper						
Dirty						
Beat						
Flower						
Hate						
Dead						
Iron						
Spin						
Wrong						
Water						
House						
Happy						
Bite						
Slate						
Stroke						

Table 1:60

Stimulus	Response	Time	S	L	R	F
Feed						
Against						
Thin						
Blue						
Small						
Box						
Strong						
Kill						
Cloth						
Write						
Boy						
Rope						
Gentle						
Silly						
Dance						
Nice						
Wrap						
Dress						
Sick						
Solve						
Point						
Kiss						
Storm						
Mutton						

Table 1:61

Stimulus	Response	Time	S	L	R	F
Cook	Food	0.3	√		√	
Red	Flag	2.0		√	√	
Smooth	Rough	1.3	√		√	
Below	Above	3.5		√	√	
Baby	Mother	0.6	√		√	
Grope	Feel	2.3		√		√
Car	Wheel	0.8	√			√
Jewel	Brooch	1.3	√			√
Alone	Lonely	0.9	√		√	
Paper	Pen	0.9	√			√
Dirty	Clean	0.5	√			√
Beat	Smack	0.7	√			√
Flower	Petal	3.2		√	√	
Hate	Love	0.9	√			√
Dead	Alive	2.1		√	√	
Iron	Mongery	1.4	√			√
Spin	Wheel	1.9		√	√	
Wrong	Right	1.3	√			√
Water	Fire	3.1		√		√
House	Door	1.2	√			√
Happy	Sad	1.8		√	√	
Bite	Food	2.1		√		√
Slate	Roof	3.1		√		√
Stroke	Cat	1.7		√		√
			13	11	10	14

Table 1:62

Stimulus	Response	Time	S	L	R	F
Feed	Food	0.6	√		√	
Against	Far	0.7	√			√
Thin	Fat	1.8		√	√	
Blue	Bell	2.6		√	√	
Small	Stone	1.2	√			√
Box	Chocolates	1.2	√		√	
Strong	Man	0.9	√			√
Kill	Death	2.6		√	√	
Cloth	Material	1.7		√	√	
Write	Paper	2.2		√	√	
Boy	Girl	1.6		√	√	
Rope	Swing	1.3	√			√
Gentle	Baby	1.4	√			√
Silly	Joke	1.8		√		√
Dance	College	1.7		√	√	
Nice	Horrible	0.8	√			√
Wrap	Cloak	1.9		√		√
Dress	Style	0.7	√			√
Sick	Illness	3.0		√	√	
Solve	Problem	1.1	√			√
Point	Pencil	0.8	√			√
Kiss	Boy	1.2	√			√
Storm	Rain•	4.0		√		√
Mutton	Sleeve	0.9	√			√
			13	11	10	14

Pages 178—179 show the responses and response times of a subject together with a record of S, L, R and F. Using the data on those sheets the appropriate statistical analysis is made using chi-square with Yates' Correction (see Appendix 2, Treatment 7, p. 205). This subject's results are classified as follows:

	(S) Short response latency		(L) Long response latency	
Subject	(R) Recalled	(F) Forgotten	(R) Recalled	(F) Forgotten
J. Edwards	6	20	14	8

The frequency observed table would therefore be:

(O)

	(S)	(L)	Total
(R)	6	14	20
(F)	20	8	28
Total	26	22	48

$$\chi^2 = 6.48 \quad \text{d.f. 1} \quad p < 0.05$$

Summary

The results indicate that this particular subject has a significantly greater ability to recall L than S response latency stimuli. Long response latency (LRL) could be caused either by the suppression of an unpleasant association and the substitution of a more acceptable one, or by the fact that the stimulus word produces a number of associations from which the subject must make his choice. In either case, it is probably reasonable to suppose that LRL stimulus words have a greater emotional significance for the subject and, assuming this to be true, this subject's results would also seem to indicate that those words which produce a stronger emotional response are more easily recalled.

When this experiment is conducted with a number of subjects and experimenters, results occur which indicate high recall levels for either LRL as above, or SRL. In other words, subjects tend to be either predominantly SRL recallers or LRL recallers. Also, the incidence of SRL or LRL can be considerably higher than those shown in the worked example.

Sometimes these differences can be attributed to differences between experimenters, i.e. some may develop in their subjects a set for the quick response but others may not. However, when one experimenter deals with a succession of subjects, this overall bias toward either SRL or LRL still persists. A possible explanation for this may be fundamental differences in the cognitive styles of the subjects, and if we take Kagan's (1971) model of reflective and impulsive cognitive styles we may have some possible explanation for these differences. He suggests that some subjects pause to evaluate the quality and accuracy of their responses, and mentally analyse their ideas and censor many possible solutions before they ever report or act upon them. This cognitive style is called reflective. Other subjects, of equal ability, accept and report the first idea they think of with minimal consideration of its appropriateness or quality. This cognitive style is termed 'impulsive'. He suggests further that there are differences in the accuracy of recall between matched subjects with these different cognitive styles. Kagan also suggests that the major cause of respective attitude is anxiety over making a mistake, whereas the impulsive subject does not seem similarly upset about mistakes.

Further applications

1   Examine the relationship between response latency and neuroticism on the Eysenck Personality Inventory (see overview of this section).

2   Examine the relationship between response latency and selected factors (e.g. Q_3, 0) on Cattell's 16 PF (see overview of this section).

3   For other uses of the word association test and a detailed discussion of alternative methods of rating and analysing responses see Andreas (1960).

References

ANDREAS, B. G. Experimental Psychology, John Wiley, 1960.
KAGAN, J. Understanding Children: Behavior, Motives, and Thought, Harcourt, Brace, Jovanovich, 1971.
WOODWORTH, R. S., & SCHLOSBERG, H. Experimental Psychology, Methuen, London, 1966.

INDIVIDUAL DIFFERENCES

Most of the experiments in this book have investigated phenomena which are characteristics of groups of people. It was seen that many people held stereotyped views of others, that human memory seemed to be similarly organized in all people, and that the efficiency with which anyone learns can be greatly influenced by manipulating various aspects of the learning situation. During the experiments the reader may also have been aware that there were other characteristics of performance which were not common to the group. These are termed *individual differences*, and a good deal of psychology is taken up with their investigation.

In the field of learning it is now expected that the sexes may show quite distinct differences in behaviour. Even more recently a rather complex relationship between sex and personality seems to be appearing (see the summary by Entwistle, 1972). Yet less than a decade ago it was usually considered legitimate for a researcher to treat a sample of students or schoolchildren as a homogeneous group of 'subjects'.

This tendency is less true of social psychology. It has long been assumed that the socialization processes through which boys and girls pass are different in some significant respects (see Danziger, 1971). The stereotype of the 'good, sweet, ladylike' little girl and the 'rough, tough, devil-may-care' little boy lead to quite different demands being made upon the two sexes during their formative years. It is now felt that rather than this being evidence of a fundamental difference in the constitution of the sexes, it may be an interesting case of a self-fulfilling prophecy. If parents assert that boys and girls have different behavioural patterns they will then treat them in such a way that these patterns emerge. The crucial question is, did differences exist *before* the children were treated differently, or would they have emerged if both sexes had been treated the same way? Experiment 19, 'need for achievement', indicated that sex differences may be expected to influence academic motivation. It is interesting to speculate upon the origins of these differences.

There are other differences between people which can easily be demonstrated. Experiment 20 'differences in taste perception', showed that some people perceive a strong taste from PTC when other perceive nothing. It is known that this ability to taste the substance is controlled by a single dominant gene, and is therefore a subject of great interest to the geneticist. It may be that there are other perceptual differences which may be of great psychological importance. In any case it is sobering to discover just how lacking in objectivity our perceptions are.

Corcoran (1964) discovered that there were individual differences in people's salivatory responses to lemon juice, and that these were closely related to the personality trait of extraversion. This was a small part of the evidence which led Eysenck (1967) to conclude that extraverts and introverts differed, not only in observable dispositions, but also in certain neurological mechanisms.

There are many ways in which to attempt a classification of human personality, and a variety of techniques with which to do it. The most frequently used method is probably the 'inventory' method. An inventory consisting of a large number of written statements is presented to the subject, who is asked to record whether he agrees or disagrees with them as accurate assessments of his behaviour and feelings. The responses are scored and the subject rated on whatever dimensions the inventory measures. The Eysenck Personality Inventory (Eysenck & Eysenck, 1964) rates subjects on two scales, extraversion and neuroticism, and Cattell's 16 PF (Cattell, 1949) does a similar thing on a range of 16 inter-related personality factors. Continued research in this field may enable us eventually to predict a person's behaviour in a given situation, not only in terms of the situational variables, but also in the interaction of these with individual personality variables.

Experiment 21, 'response latencies', draws attention to another area which has received a good deal of attention lately, that of 'impulsive' and 'reflective' cognitive styles. Work by Kagan (1963 & 1971) suggests that the tendency to respond to a task in a quick, impulsive manner, or in a slow, reflective way, is a stable characteristic of the individual in a variety of situations. Educators are beginning to realize the importance of such an individual difference, for the reflective child placed with a teacher who sees rapid answers as indicative of alertness may be most unfortunate.

The empirical social sciences will no doubt continue to define areas of individual difference, and devise methods of assessing them. In each case the analysis is an attempt to define the highly individual nature of each subject from one particular perspective. Whether the sum total of such endeavours will ever add up to an accurate representation of the individual, offering unequivocal predictions of behaviour in a given situation, is a matter for conjecture.

References

CATTELL, R. B., & STICE, G. The Sixteen Personality Factor Questionnaire, Institute of Personality & Ability Testing, 1949.
CORCORAN, D. W. J. The Relation Between Introversion and Salivation, American Journal of Psychology, 2, 77, pp. 298–300, 1964.
DANZIGER, K. Socialization, Penguin, London, 1971.
ENTWISTLE, N. J. Personality and Academic Attainment, British Journal of Educational Psychology, 2, 42, pp. 137–151, 1972.
EYSENCK, H. J., & EYSENCK, S. B. G. Eysenck Personality Inventory, Educational and Industrial Testing Service, 1964.
EYSENCK, H. J. & EYSENCK, S. B. G. On the Unitary Nature of Extraversion, Acta Psychologica, 26, pp. 383–390, 1967.
KAGAN, J. Understanding Children: Behavior, Motives and Thought. Harcourt, Brace & Jovanovich, 1971.
KAGAN, J., MOSS, H. A., & SIGEL, I. E. Psychological Significance of Styles of Thinking, in J. C. Wright & J. Kagan (Eds.) Basic Cognitive Processes in Children, Monograph of Society for Research in Child Development, 28, 2, pp. 73–112, 1963.

Details for the Construction of the Maze for Experiment 15

Take a plain 12 in. (30 cm) polystyrene ceiling tile and draw a maze based on the specimen shown in Figure A1:1. Care should be taken not to construct a maze having a correct route which consists of only right-hand or only left-hand turns. Also there should not be more than 12 blind alleys.

The channels, drawn on the tile, should be 0.5 in. (3 mm) wide. These channels should be carefully cut out, using a razor or a battery-heated wire element cutter. If money and equipment allow, more durable mazes can be constructed using squares of hardboard, wood or metal.

Figure A1:1 Maze Learning (Specimen maze)

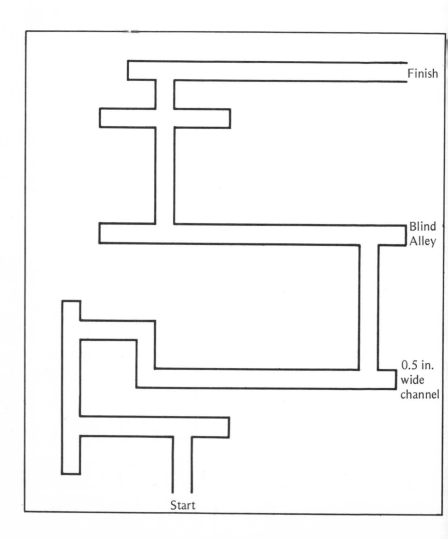

Details for the Construction of the Moveable List Viewing Frame for Experiments 13 and 17

Figure A1:2 Construction of Viewing Frame

1   Fold a sheet of foolscap paper in
     half lengthwise

2   Fold in half the other way making
     a fold 'a'

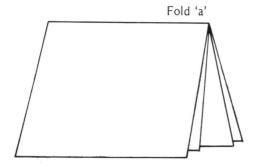

3 Mark out a rectangle along fold 'a'
and cut it out (through four thick-
nesses of paper)

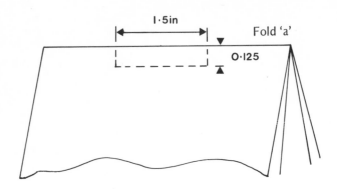

4 Open out to a single folded sheet
with a 1.5 x 0.25 in. slot

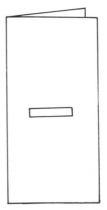

5   Place the list of words in the
    frame

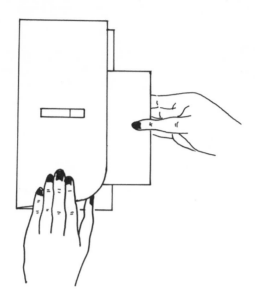

6   Move the list upwards as instruc-
    ted

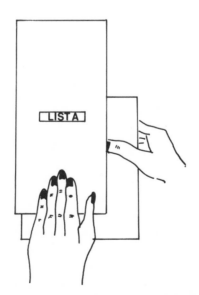

Statistical Procedures for Analysing Data from these Experiments

2a Objectives of this appendix

Real understanding and appreciation of mathematical statistics requires a considerable amount of mathematical training. This appendix merely sets out (to paraphrase Moroney, 1951) to give the reader a selective, conducted, tour of the statistician's workshop. The reader is shown a selection of tools and given a brief explanation of their purpose, method of operation and demonstration of use; then, under strict supervision, is allowed to try for himself.

Reference

MORONEY, M. J., Facts from Figures, Pelican, 1951.

2b Introduction to measurement

Much of the experimentation in this book is aimed at finding functional relationships between independent and dependent variables. An independent variable is one which is being systematically varied by the experimenter whereas a dependent variable is one not directly under the experimenter's control. To examine relationships between these variables is the object of our investigations.

In our experiments, all the variables are entities which are measurable, i.e. they may increase or decrease along a given continuum. Since all our experimental data are obtained by using some type of measurement technique, it is important first to consider what measurement is and, secondly, to become acquainted with the several different kinds of measurement by which we quantify behaviour. These behavioural measurements can subsequently be treated statistically so that we can obtain an orderly quantitative description of the behaviour, and it is important to understand that the statistical procedure is selected according to the type of measurement scale used.

The most common definition of measurement seems to be that measurement is the assigning of numbers to things according to rules. Measurement transforms certain characteristics of our perceptions into familiar, amenable things called 'numbers'. The general formulation of different kinds, or levels, of measurement that has been most useful to behavioural scientists is the one set up by Stevens (1951). According to this system, we can divide the possible ways of assigning numerals into four scale types each of which has rules and restrictions of its own, which is why only certain statistical procedures are appropriate in each case. These four scales are hierarchical, i.e. there is a progression from a low scale to a high scale and each higher scale incorporates all the properties of the lower.

The first and lowest of these scales is the *nominal* scale. This is used when numbers are assigned only to identify the categories to which individual persons or things belong, e.g. nationalities or car licence-plate numbers. It can also be used to label groups of persons, as when men are given the code number '1' and women the code number '0'. The only arithmetic use to which this scale's numbers can be put is counting. The numerals should never be added, subtracted, multiplied or divided.

The second level of measurement is the *ordinal* scale. This measure incorporates the information given by the previous scale by categorizing and labelling but adds to it a sense of order. We use this scale to arrange individuals in a series ranging from the highest to the lowest according to the characteristics we wish to measure. We cannot say, however, exactly how much difference exists between any two of them. For example, we could rate a group of people on friendliness and list them from highest to lowest. There is, however, no assumption that the difference in degree of friendliness between Subjects 2 and 3 is the same as between Subjects 5 and 6; nor is there any assumption that the first person is twice as friendly as the second person or ten times as friendly as the tenth person. In addition to the procedures allowed for the nominal scale, the ordinal scale allows ranking methods and statistical procedures based on interpretations of 'greater than' and 'less than'.

The third level of measurement is the *interval* scale. The title of this scale describes its additional quality, i.e. the interval scale permits us to state just how far apart two people or things are. Most educational tests are of this type. Although there may be some doubt about their measurement properties, most teachers regard scores on course examinations as interval scales. Teachers would consider it reasonable to compare the scores of two pupils and describe one as having ten marks less than the other. But interval scores do have the limitation of having no real zero point. For example, a zero score on any school test does not automatically imply that the pupil has no knowledge whatsoever of the subject tested. It is not necessary, however, to define zero knowledge in school tests, since their aim is usually to compare pupils with one another. In addition to the arithmetic procedures allowed with the lower scales, an interval score can be added or subtracted and statistical procedures based on these operations may be used.

The final and highest level of measurement is the *ratio* scale, which yields the most information. It includes an absolute zero, provides equal intervals, gives an order, and can be used for simple labelling. However, very few educational or psychological tests provide ratio scale scores, since they would need an absolute zero — which would mean, for example, zero intelligence or personality scores. The physical sciences, however, make great use of ratio scales with absolute zeros such as time, weight, and length. Using length as an illustration of a ratio scale we can say that no material at all is a zero measure, that a 12 ft long length is 8 ft longer than a 4 ft length and, in ratio terms, it is also reasonable to describe it as three times as long as a 4 ft length.

The experiments in this text use data obtained from these four scales, and the statistical treatments used to analyse the data are carefully selected for their appropriateness. This appendix is not sufficiently comprehensive to enable the lay reader to apply these treatments to other experimental situations without first acquiring, through careful training, real understanding and appreciation of mathematical statistics.

Reference

STEVENS, S. S. *Handbook of Experimental Psychology*, Wiley, New York, 1951.

2c Calculating procedures for the various statistical treatments

Treatment 1

The Mean $(\bar{X})$ (used in Experiments 7, 10, 12, 13, 14, 16 and 19).

The mean $(\bar{X})$ is a measure used to describe the central tendency of a distribution of measurements for a group, and it is the main statistic used to describe the average value of a set of scores. It is calculated by dividing the total number of scores (ΣX) by the total number of observations (N).

The formula is expressed as follows:

$$\bar{X} \text{ (the mean)} = \frac{\Sigma X}{N}$$

The calculating procedure is demonstrated using the scores obtained by Group 1 in Experiment 10 (p. 108).

Group 1

2

4

8

2

7

6

7

7

$\Sigma X = 43$ $\quad N = 8$

$\dfrac{43}{8} = 5.38$

$\bar{X} = 5.38$

The mean is by far the most used and familiar index of central tendency for a set of raw data. For a detailed description concerning the interpretation of means consult Glass and Stanley (1970).

Reference

GLASS, G. V. and STANLEY, J. C. Statistical Methods in Education and Psychology, Prentice-Hall, 1970.

The Median (Mdn) (used in Experiments 6, 8, 18).

Median (Mdn) is simply the middle score in a distribution of scores, or the number that would represent a point between the two middle ones. The median for a set of observed data is ordinarily defined in slightly different ways depending upon whether the sample size (N) is odd or even. When (N) is odd the median corresponds to the score of individual number $(N + 1)/2$ when all individuals are arranged in order by scores; when (N) is even, the median is defined as the score-value midway between the scores for individual

$\dfrac{N}{2}$ and individual $\dfrac{N}{2} + 1$ in order.

Computation of the median from raw data

The median is simply that *point* on a scale of measurement above which there are exactly half the scores and below which there are the other half of the scores.

In the distribution 1, 3, 5, 7, 9, 11, 13, the middle score is 7. Thus the score of 7 indicates the median *point* at which there are 3 scores above and 3 scores below.

The median is obtained by arranging the scores in ascending order from the smallest to the highest score and selecting that point above and below which there are an equal number of scores. The median point in a distribution of scores the total of which comes to an odd number, is the middle score in that distribution providing of course that the middle score has a frequency of one. When the middle score in a distribution has a frequency of more than one then one needs to understand the meaning of the *interval of a score* in order to calculate the median point.

The *interval of a score* defines the exact limits of that score and ranges from 0.50 units below to 0.50 units above that score. Thus the score of 3 includes all values within the limits of 2.50 to 3.50. The exact midpoint of the interval having lower and upper limits ranging from 2.50 to 3.50, is 3.

Look at the distribution below

$$2, 3, 3, 4, 5, 5, 5, 7, 9, 10$$
$$\uparrow$$

The score of 5 has a frequency of 3. The exact limits (the interval range of 5) includes all values from 4.50 to 5.50. We take it that the scores 5, 5, 5 are spread equally through the interval of 4.50 to 5.50. Thus each 5 occupies 1/3 (0.33) of that interval, as shown in the diagram below

$$: \quad 5 \quad : \quad 5 \quad : \quad 5 \quad :$$
$$4.50 \quad\quad 4.83 \quad\quad 5.16 \quad\quad 5.50$$

The median point of the distribution 2, 3, 3, 4, 5, 5, 5, 7, 9, 10 is located between the fifth and the sixth scores. Below the interval 4.50 to 5.50 there are four scores (2,3,3,4). The fifth score (5) is thus 1/3 of the distance into the interval 4.50 to 5.50, that is 4.50 + 0.33 = 4.83. The median is shown in the diagram

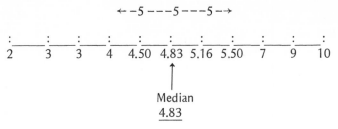

Look at the distribution below

3, 4, 4, 5, 5, 5, 5, 6, 7.

There is an odd number of scores in the distribution and the median is located at the point indicated by the arrow, that is, within a group of four 5s. We take it that the scores 5, 5, 5, 5 are spread equally throughout the interval 4.50 to 5.50. Thus each 5 occupies 1/4 (0.25) of the interval as shown in the diagram below

```
    5   5   5   5
:___:___:___:___:
4.50 4.75 5.00 5.25 5.50
```

In the diagram below showing the total distribution, the median is located midpoint between 4.75 and 5.00, that is at a point 4.75 + 1/2 (0.25) = 4.875 (4.88)

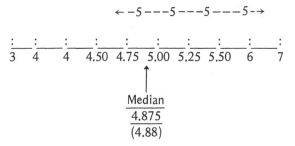

Look at the distribution below

53, 54, 55, 59, 62, 67, 70, 71

The median is located between the fourth and the fifth score, that is at a point between the upper exact limit of 59 (59.50) and the lower exact limit of 62 (61.50). The diagram below locates the median at 60.5.

```
:___:___:___:___:___:___:
59  59.50 60 60.50 61 61.50 62
          ↑
        Median
        60.50
```

For a description of the median as a measure of central tendency see Hays (1969).

Reference

HAYS, W. L., *Statistics*, Holt, Rinehart & Winston, New York, 1969.

The Standard Deviation (s.d.) (used in experiments 7, 10, 12, 13, 14, 16, 19).

The s.d. gives us an indication of the variability of scores within a group. It gives a valuable shorthand way of comparing groups and individuals within groups. The formula for calculating the s.d. is as follows:

$$\text{s.d.} = \sqrt{\frac{\Sigma d^2}{N}}$$

The steps in the calculation of the s.d. are as follows:

1   Calculate the mean of the set of scores.

2   Calculate the differences between the several scores and their mean.

3   Calculate the squares of these differences. (The square of a number is found by multiplying it by itself. Thus, the square of 4 is written 4^2 and has the value of 4 x 4 = 16.)

4   Calculate the sum of squares of the differences to get a quantity known as the 'sample sum of squares'.

5   Divide this sample sum of squares by the number of items, n, in the set of scores. This gives a quantity known as the sample variance.

6   Take the square root of the variance and so obtain the s.d.

The calculation is demonstrated using the scores obtained by Group 1 in Experiment 10 (p. 110).

Group 1 scores

X difference from mean (X)	differences^2 (d^2)
2 − 3.38	11.42
4 − 1.38	1.90
8 2.62	6.86
2 − 3.38	11.42
7 1.62	2.62
6 0.62	0.38
7 1.62	2.62
7 1.62	2.62
$\Sigma X = 43$	Σd^2 39.84

$\bar{X} = 5.38$

$N = 8$

$$\text{s.d.} = \sqrt{\frac{39.84}{8}} = \sqrt{4.98} = 2.23$$

For a full discussion of the uses of the s.d. and its relationship to the normal curve of distribution consult Blommers and Lindquist (1960).

Reference

BLOMMERS, P., and LINDQUIST, E. F., Elementary Statistical Methods in Psychology and Education, University of London Press, 1960.

The t Test (t) (used in Experiments 7, 10, 12, 14, 16, 19.)

This test is appropriate for determining whether the means of two samples differ so much that the samples are unlikely to be drawn from the same population. Its use assumes interval measurement, approximately normal population distribution of the underlying variable and approximately equal variances in the two populations being compared.

The exact formula for t varies according to circumstances. The following are two formulae appropriate for testing differences between means of large samples and small samples.

(a) The formula for calculating a t test between the means of two large samples is as follows:

$$t = \frac{\bar{X}_1 - \bar{X}_2}{\sqrt{\dfrac{\text{s.d.}_1^2}{n_1} + \dfrac{\text{s.d.}_2^2}{n_2}}}$$

This test is appropriate for samples like those in Experiments 7 and 19. Using the data given on p. 79, (Experiment 7), the calculating procedure is as follows:

1   Calculate the mean (X) for each group (see Treatment 1, p. 190).
2   Calculate the s.d. for each group (see Treatment 3, p. 194).

Group 1   Group 2

$\bar{X}_1 = 11.31$ $\bar{X}_2 = 8.76$

$\text{s.d.}_1 = 2.40$ $\text{s.d.}_2 = 3.42$

$n_1 = 63$ $n_2 = 65$

$\bar{X}_1 - \bar{X}_2 = 11.31 - 8.76 = 2.55$

$$\sqrt{\frac{\text{s.d.}_1^2}{n_1} + \frac{\text{s.d.}_2^2}{n_2}} = \sqrt{\frac{5.76}{63} + \frac{11.69}{65}} = \sqrt{0.27} = 0.52$$

Hence, $t = \dfrac{2.55}{0.52} = 4.9$

The number of degrees of freedom is $(n_1 - 1) + (n_2 - 1)$ which in this example is $62 + 64 = 126$.

The d.f. is used to indicate the value of t required for a significant difference between the means. We refer the d.f. to Table A2.10 and read off the significance levels. Since the d.f. is so large, we would use the infinity sign (∞) as our indicator. Our t result (4.9) is greater than the 0.05 or 0.01 levels so we can infer a significant difference between the means.

(b) Where we wish to compare the means of small samples of less than 50 observations, the use of the preceding formula is no longer appropriate. The test is similar but corrections have been made to allow for sampling errors which are more important in small samples.

Formula:

$$t = \frac{(\bar{X}_1 - \bar{X}_2)\sqrt{\dfrac{1}{N}}}{\sqrt{\Sigma(x_1^2) - \dfrac{(\Sigma(x_1)^2)}{n_1} + \Sigma(x_2^2) - \dfrac{(\Sigma(x_2)^2}{n_2}}}$$

d.f. in this case are calculated as follows:

$$n_1 + n_2 - 2$$

This method of calculating t should be used with sample sizes like those in Experiments 10, 12, 14 and 16.

Experiment 10 gives us data for two small samples. The procedure for calculating t in this case is as follows:

Group 1		Group 2	
x_1	x_1^2	x_2	x_2^2
2	4	9	81
4	16	8	64
8	64	9	81
2	4	8	64
7	49	8	64
6	36	4	16
7	49	7	49
7	49	10	100
43	271	63	519

$$n = 8 \qquad\qquad n = 8$$
$$\Sigma(x_1) = 43 \qquad \Sigma(x_2) = 63$$
$$\Sigma(x_1^2) = 271 \qquad \Sigma(x_2^2) = 519$$
$$\bar{X}_1 = 5.38 \qquad \bar{X}_2 = 7.87$$

$$\bar{x}_2 - \bar{x}_1 = 7.87 - 5.38 = 2.49$$

$$\sqrt{\frac{8 \times 8 \times 14}{16}} = \sqrt{\frac{896}{16}} = \sqrt{56} = 7.48$$

$$271 - \frac{1,849}{8} + 519 - \frac{3,969}{8}$$

$$= 271 - 231.13 + 519 - 496.13$$

$$= 39.87 + 22.87 = 62.74$$

$$t = \frac{2.49 \times 7.48}{\sqrt{62.74}} = \frac{2.49 \times 7.48}{7.92} = \frac{18.62}{7.92} = 2.35$$

$$\text{d.f.} = n_1 + n_2 - 2 = 8 + 8 - 2 = 14.$$

The value of t on Table A2.10 at 0.05 level is 2.145. Since our calculated t is greater than this we may conclude that the difference between means is significant.

For an extended discussion on the uses and limitations of t, readers should consult Edwards (1967).

Reference

EDWARDS, A. L., *Statistical Methods for the Behavioral Sciences*, Holt Rinehart and Winston, 1967.

Analysis of Variance (ANOVA) (used in Experiment 13).

Analysis of variance (ANOVA) is a hypothesis-testing technique and is concerned with the basic question: 'Do these means differ significantly?' There are various forms of analysis of variance and many refinements of the basic model. For a useful general discussion of the uses of analysis of variance see Chapter 11 in Connolly and Sluckin (1962), but for a deep and detailed account of analysis of variance and its refined uses, readers should consult Glass and Stanley (1970) Chapters 15 to 17 and Chapter 19.

In Experiment 13 we are concerned to test for differences in level of recall on three lists of equal length. Using the data given in Experiment 13 the calculating procedure is as follows:

ANALYSIS OF RESULTS

Scores x

Groups	1	2	3	
	16	11	9	
	20	18	18	
	20	12	10	
	16	16	15	
	20	20	10	
	20	20	17	
	17	19	15	
	16	16	16	
	16	19	16	
	20	20	13	
	20	20	13	
	20	20	13	
	221	211	165	= 597

Squared scores x^2

Groups	1	2	3	
	256	121	81	
	400	324	324	
	400	144	100	
	256	256	225	
	400	400	100	
	400	400	289	
	289	361	225	
	256	256	256	
	256	361	256	
	400	400	169	
	400	400	169	
	400	400	169	
	4,113	3,823	2,363	= 10,299

1 Total sum of squares

$$\Sigma\Sigma x = 597$$

$$\Sigma\Sigma x^2 = 10{,}299$$

$$\frac{(\Sigma\Sigma x)^2}{N} = \frac{356{,}409}{36} = 9{,}900$$

$$\Sigma\Sigma x^2 - \frac{(\Sigma\Sigma x)^2}{N} \quad 10{,}299 - 9{,}900 = 399$$

2 Sum of squares within groups

$$\Sigma x^2 - \frac{\Sigma x}{n_1} \text{ (Group 1)} + \Sigma x^2 - \frac{\Sigma x}{n_2} \text{ (Group 2)} + \Sigma x^2 - \frac{\Sigma x}{n_3} \text{ (Group 3)}$$

$$4{,}113 - \frac{221^2}{12} + 3{,}823 - \frac{211^2}{12} + 2{,}363 - \frac{165^2}{12} = 250$$

3 Sum of squares between groups

Total sum of squares	= 399
Sum of squares within groups	= 250
Sum of squares between groups	= 149

4 Cross-check

$$\text{Sum of squares between} = \frac{221^2 + 211^2 + 165^2}{12} - 9{,}900 = 149$$

5 Analysis of variance

	Sum of squares	d.f	Mean square	F
Between groups	149	No. of Groups − 1 = 2	74.5 *2	9.84 *4
Within groups	250	$(N_1 - 1) + (n_2 - 1) + (n_3 - 1)$ = 33	7.57 *3	
Totals	399	$N - 1 = 35$ *1		

Notes:
*1 If less than 100, otherwise N
*2 Mean square = sum of squares between ÷ d.f. between
*3 Mean square = sum of squares within ÷ d.f. within
*4 F = mean square between ÷ mean square within

Significance is then checked using an F table (see Tables A2.11, A2.12). F = 5.39 at 0.01 level. 9.84 exceeds this and there is, therefore, less than one chance in a 100 that the differences occurred by chance.

References

CONNOLLY, T. G., and SLUCKIN, W. *Statistics for the Social Sciences*, Cleaver-Hume, 1962.
GLASS, G. V., and STANLEY, J. C. *Statistical Methods in Education and Psychology*, Prentice-Hall, 1970.

Kruskal—Wallis One-Way Analysis of Variance by Ranks (used in Experiments 6 and 8)

The Kruskal—Wallis one-way analysis of variance by ranks is an appropriate test for deciding whether a number of independent samples are from different populations or whether differences among those samples are due to variations that might be expected to occur by chance among samples drawn randomly from the same population.

In the example in Experiment 6, we are concerned with the role conflict scores of three independent samples of student teachers. The median scores of each of the three samples are placed in rank order. That is to say, the median scores of all three student groups are simultaneously ranked from lowest to highest, the smallest median score being assigned Rank 1, the next smallest median score Rank 2 and so on. These ranks are then summed to obtain R_1, R_2 and R_3 shown at the bottom of Table 1.9 (p. 59). H, the statistic used in the Kruskal—Wallis test is defined by the formula:

$$H = \frac{12}{N(N+1)} \frac{R_j^2}{n_j} - 3(N+1)$$

where N = the number of cases in all samples combined (in our example $N = 30$, i.e. the total number of role conflict median scores).

$$\frac{R_j^2}{n_j} = \frac{R_1^2}{n_1} + \frac{R_2^2}{n_2} + \frac{R_3^2}{n_3} \ldots$$

$$H = \frac{12}{30(30+1)} \left(\frac{159^2}{10} + \frac{145^2}{10} + \frac{161^2}{10} \right) - 3(30+1)$$

$$H = \left(\frac{12}{930} \times 7222.7 \right) - 93$$

$$H = 0.19$$

The significance of H (small samples)

Where there are small numbers of cases in each of the samples (less than five cases) the significance of H may be obtained by reference to Table A2:1, (p. 203).

The significance of H (large samples)

Where there are more than five cases in each of the samples (as in the present example) the significance of H is obtained by reference to the chi-square Table A2:13 on p. 234. Degrees of freedom are determined by d.f. = $K - 1$ where K is the number of independent samples (in the present example, the three student groups).

From Table A2:13 (p. 234) a value of 5.99 (d.f. = 2) is required for H to be significant at the 0.05 level. Clearly, the value obtained, 0.19, indicates that in respect of their role conflict scores our three student groups must be assumed to have been drawn from the same population. That is, there are no significant differences between them.

Table of Probabilities Associated with Values as Large as Observed Values of H in the Kruskal–Wallis One-Way Analysis of Variance by Ranks (5 or less cases in each of the samples)

n_1	n_2	n_3	H	p	n_1	n_2	n_3	H	p
2	1	1	2.7000	0.500	4	3	2	6.4444	0.008
								6.3000	0.011
2	2	1	3.6000	0.200				5.4444	0.046
								5.4000	0.051
2	2	2	4.5714	0.067				4.5111	0.098
			3.7143	0.200				4.4444	0.102
3	1	1	3.2000	0.300					
					4	3	3	6.7455	0.010
3	2	1	4.2857	0.100				6.7091	0.013
			3.8571	0.133				5.7909	0.046
								5.7273	0.050
3	2	2	5.3572	0.029				4.7091	0.092
			4.7143	0.048				4.7000	0.101
			4.5000	0.067	4	4	1	6.6667	0.010
			4.4643	0.105				6.1667	0.022
3	3	1	5.1429	0.043				4.9667	0.048
			4.5714	0.100				4.8667	0.054
			4.0000	0.129				4.1667	0.082
3	3	2	6.2500	0.011				4.0667	0.102
			5.3611	0.032					
			5.1389	0.061	4	4	2	7.0364	0.006
			4.5556	0.100				6.8727	0.011
			4.2500	0.121				5.4545	0.046
								5.2364	0.052
3	3	3	7.2000	0.004				4.5545	0.098
			6.4889	0.011				4.4455	0.103
			5.6889	0.029					
			5.6000	0.050	4	4	3	7.1439	0.010
			5.0667	0.086				7.1364	0.011
			4.6222	0.100				5.5985	0.049
								5.5758	0.051
4	1	1	3.5714	0.200				4.5455	0.099
								4.4773	0.102
4	2	1	4.8214	0.057					
			4.5000	0.076	4	4	4	7.6538	0.008
			4.0179	0.114				7.5385	0.011
4	2	2	6.0000	0.014				5.6923	0.049
			5.3333	0.033				5.6538	0.054
			5.1250	0.052				4.6539	0.097
			4.4583	0.100				4.5001	0.104
			4.1667	0.105	5	1	1	3.8571	0.143
4	3	1	5.8333	0.021	5	2	1	5.2500	0.036
			5.2083	0.050				5.0000	0.048
			5.0000	0.057				4.4500	0.071
			4.0556	0.093				4.2000	0.095
			3.8889	0.129				4.0500	0.119

Sample sizes			H	p
n_1	n_2	n_3		
5	2	2	6.5333	0.008
			6.1333	0.013
			5.1600	0.034
			5.0400	0.056
			4.3733	0.090
			4.2933	0.122
5	3	1	6.4000	0.012
			4.9600	0.048
			4.8711	0.052
			4.0178	0.095
			3.8400	0.123
5	3	2	6.9091	0.009
			6.8218	0.010
			5.2509	0.049
			5.1055	0.052
			4.6509	0.091
			4.4945	0.101
5	3	3	7.0788	0.009
			6.9818	0.011
			5.6485	0.049
			5.5152	0.051
			4.5333	0.097
			4.4121	0.109
5	4	1	6.9545	0.008
			6.8400	0.011
			4.9855	0.044
			4.8600	0.056
			3.9873	0.098
			3.9600	0.102
5	4	2	7.2045	0.009
			7.1182	0.010
			5.2727	0.049
			5.2682	0.050
			4.5409	0.098
			4.5182	0.101
5	4	3	7.4449	0.010
			7.3949	0.011
			5.6564	0.049

Samples sizes			H	p
n_1	n_2	n_3		
			5.6308	0.050
			4.5487	0.099
			4.5231	0.103
5	4	4	7.7604	0.009
			7.7440	0.011
			5.6571	0.049
			5.6176	0.050
			4.6187	0.100
			4.5527	0.102
5	5	1	7.3091	0.009
			6.8364	0.011
			5.1273	0.046
			4.9091	0.053
			4.1091	0.086
			4.0364	0.105
5	5	2	7.3385	0.010
			7.2692	0.010
			5.3385	0.047
			5.2462	0.051
			4.6231	0.097
			4.5077	0.100
5	5	3	7.5780	0.010
			7.5429	0.010
			5.7055	0.046
			5.6264	0.051
			4.5451	0.100
			4.5363	0.102
5	5	4	7.8229	0.010
			7.7914	0.010
			5.6657	0.049
			5.6429	0.050
			4.5229	0.099
			4.5200	0.101
5	5	5	8.0000	0.009
			7.9800	0.010
			5.7800	0.049
			5.6600	0.051
			4.5600	0.100
			4.5000	0.102

By courtesy of:
'Non-Parametric Statistics' by S. S. Siegel (c), 1956, McGraw-Hill Book Company Inc. Reproduced by permission.

The Chi-Square Test (χ^2) (used in experiments 1, 2, 4, 5, 7, 8, 19, 21).

The χ^2 test is designed primarily to deal with hypotheses that concern data in the nominal form and when you calculate χ^2 on your data, the following rules of thumb should apply. For tables with more than a single d.f. (larger than 2 x 2 cells) a minimum expected frequency of five can be regarded as adequate, but when there is only a single d.f. a minimum expected frequency of ten is much safer. Yates' correction should be used on tables of data which have one d.f. (i.e. 2 x 2 tables).

Experiment 1 provides the data for a demonstration of the calculation of χ^2 and as such provides a model for subsequent χ^2 analyses used in Experiments 2, 4, 5, 7. The formula for χ^2 is as follows:

$$\chi^2 = \sum \frac{(O-E)^2}{E}$$

Using the specimen results in Experiment 1 we would calculate χ^2 using the following steps:

1　This table shows the results of our observations. (O) is the observed frequency of behaviour in the various categories, e.g. 73 males absolutely stopped.

(O)

Drivers	Absolute stop	Slowed but did not stop	Total
Male	73	72	145
Female	42	19	61
Total	115	91	206

These observations are totalled in both columns and rows.

2　(E) is the frequency which would be expected to fall in each category according to our hypothesis.

(E)

Male	$\dfrac{115 \times 145}{206} = 80.95$	$\dfrac{91 \times 145}{206} = 64.05$
Female	$\dfrac{115 \times 61}{206} = 34.05$	$\dfrac{91 \times 61}{206} = 26.95$

3   The next stage in the calculation requires that we subtract the figures in the (E) table from the figures in the (O) table.

$(O-E)$

Male	7.95	7.95
Female	7.95	7.95

4   In the introduction to this statistical treatment, it was suggested that Yates' correction should be used with 2 x 2 tables which have one d.f. The d.f. for a χ^2 computed on a 2 x 2 table are calculated as follows. Rows (r) x columns (c) on the table, $(r-1)(c-1) = (2-1)(2-1) = 1 \times 1 = 1$ d.f. Similarly, d.f. for 2 x 4 tables as in Experiment 5 are calculated $(2-1)(4-1) = 1 \times 3 = 3$ d.f.

    Yates' correction consists of reducing each category in the $(O-E)$ cells by 0.5.

Thus: $(O-E)$ corrected

Male	7.45	7.45
Female	7.45	7.45

$$\frac{(O-E)^2}{E}$$

Male	$\dfrac{7.45^2}{80.95} = \dfrac{55.5}{80.95} = 0.68$	$\dfrac{7.45^2}{64.05} = \dfrac{55.5}{64.05} = 0.86$
Female	$\dfrac{7.45^2}{34.05} = \dfrac{55.5}{34.05} = 1.63$	$\dfrac{7.45^2}{26.94} = \dfrac{55.5}{26.94} = 2.06$

χ^2 = the sum of the above four cells i.e. = 5.23

Having found χ^2, its significance may be determined by consulting Table A2.13. As previously stated the d.f. total for this example is 1 and we use this to determine our distribution point on the χ^2 table. If the value of χ^2 (5.23) is as great or greater than 3.84 (1 d.f.) we may conclude that there is a significant difference between the behaviour of male and female drivers at a stop sign, i.e. the frequency distribution observed differs significantly from the frequency distribution expected. The level of significance (P) using Table A2.13 can be either at the 0.05 or 0.01 level and is sometimes expressed as $P < 0.05$ or $P < 0.01$.

Experiments 4, 5, 7 use a χ^2 test to examine the association between two variables, one of which is dichotomous, and the other capable of division into four or six classes. In each of these experiments your results may make it necessary to collapse or pool categories in order to meet the requirement of at least five in the *expected frequency* distribution of any cell. Add together only those categories which can be meaningfully joined. The calculation of χ^2 is identical to our worked example with the treatment extended to four or six cells.

A detailed discussion of the uses and limitations of χ^2 can be found in Chambers (1964), Lewis (1967) and Hays (1969).

References

CHAMBERS, E. F., *Statistical Calculations for Beginners*, (Chap. 9), Cambridge University Press, 1964.
HAYS, W. L., *Statistics*, (Chap. 17), Holt, Rinehart Winston, 1969.
LEWIS, D. G., *Statistical Methods in Education* (Chap. 9), U.L.P., 1967.

Spearman's Rank Order Correlation Coefficient
(used in Experiment 6)

Spearman's rank order correlation coefficient is an appropriate measure of association between two ranked sets of data. In the example in Experiment 6, we are concerned with the role conflict scores of two independent samples of student teachers (Years 1 and 2). Table A2:2 reproduces data shown in Experiment 6 (p. 58). The computation of Spearman's r_s is simple and straightforward. First, we take the differences of ranks (d), square those differences (d^2) and sum the squared difference (Σd^2). r_s is defined by the formula:

$$r_s = 1 - \frac{6 \Sigma (d^2)}{n(n-1)(n+1)}$$

where d = the difference in rank between the items in a pair
Σ = the sum of
n = the number of items

Table A2:2

Experiment 6: Rank orderings in role conflict by years 1 and 2 compared by Spearman's Rank Order Correlation Coefficient (r_s)

Rank ordering by Year 1		Rank ordering by Year 2			
Roles	Rank order	Roles	Rank order	d	d^2
AB	1	AB	1	0	0
AC	10	AC	8	2	4
AD	7	AD	5	2	4
AE	9	AE	6	3	9
BC	3	BC	9	6	36
BD	4	BD	7	3	9
BE	2	BE	2	0	0
CD	8	CD	10	2	4
CE	5	CE	4	1	1
DE	6	DE	3	3	9
					Σ 76

$$r_s = 1 - \frac{6 \times 76}{10(10 - 1)(10 + 1)} = 1 - \frac{456}{990}$$

$$r_s = 0.539$$

The significance of r_s may be obtained by reference to Table A2:14 (p. 234). Interpolating in that table at $n = 10$, a value of 0.564 is necessary for significance at the 0.05 level. Our value of 0.539 just falls short of that figure and we interpret our data in the light of this, namely, that the role conflict rankings of years 1 and 2 are not significantly associated.

Reference

HAYS, W. L., *Statistics*, Holt, Rinehart & Winston, New York, 1969.

t **Test of** r_s (used in Experiment 6).
The significance of r_s may be tested using the following *t* formula:

$$t = r_s \sqrt{\frac{N-2}{1-r_s^2}}$$

Using the data in Experiment 6, the calculation procedure would be as follows:

$$t = 0.539 \sqrt{\frac{10-2}{1-(0.539)^2}}$$

$$t = 0.539 \sqrt{\frac{8}{1-0.290}}$$

$$t = 0.539 \sqrt{\frac{8}{0.710}} = \sqrt{11.27} = 3.39$$

0.539 x 3.39 = 1.804

$t = 1.804$

Degrees of freedom are determined thus: d.f. $= N - 2$ where N is the number of rankings being compared. In this example, d.f. = 8, at value of 2.306 is significant of 2.306 at the 0.05 level. Our value of 1.804 is short of this figure. We can therefore conclude that our rankings are not significantly associated.

For a discussion of the use of *t* tests of correlation coefficients see Hays (1969).

Reference

HAYS, W. L., *Statistics*, Holt, Rinehart and Winston, New York, 1969.

The Phi-Coefficient (used in Experiment 19)
The formula for the phi-coefficient is as follows:

$$phi = \sqrt{\frac{\chi^2}{N}}$$

Using the data in Experiment 19 we calculate phi as we follows:

$$phi = \sqrt{\frac{\chi^2}{N}} = \sqrt{\frac{3.97}{58}} = \sqrt{0.068} = 0.26$$

The phi coefficient is used as a measure of association for a 2 x 2 contingency table. In Experiment 19 the phi coefficient (0.26) provides us with a statistic by which to describe the strength of the relationship between career choice and need for achievement. The significance of phi is taken directly from the chi-square value. Thus, if we obtain a significant value for χ^2 for the 2 x 2 table, we may also conclude that phi is significantly greater than zero.

For a full evaluation of the phi coefficient and a discussion of its reliability and significance, readers should consult Guilford (1965).

Reference

GUILFORD, J. P., *Fundamental Statistics in Psychology and Education*, McGraw-Hill Book Company Inc., Maidenhead, 1965.

An Adaptation of the McNemar Test for the Significance of Change
(used in Experiment 9)
Experiment 9 is concerned with the measurement of change in students' attitudes towards an experimental teaching method. The experiment employs a 'before and after' design in which the same subjects' evaluations are compared one with another at two different points in time. The McNemar test for the significance of change is an appropriate technique where the data (as in the present example) are at the ordinal rather than the interval level of measurement and where a 'before and after' design is employed. In the hypothetical example below, the before and after ratings of 100 subjects on the adjectival scale useful/useless have been entered in a 7 x 7 matrix to give:

Table A2:3 Adjectival scale: Useful/Useless

		Before						
		Useful						Useless
		7	6	5	4	3	2	1
Useful	7	2	10	5	1	0	0	0
	6	4	4	20	15	1	0	0
	5	1	2	3	16	0	0	0
After	4	0	1	2	4	0	0	0
	3	0	0	1	3	0	3	0
	2	0	0	0	1	0	0	0
Useless	1	0	0	0	1	0	0	0

The significance of change can be interpolated from t tables (see Table A2.10 p. 228) and is derived from the formula:

$$t = \frac{|A - D|}{\sqrt{A + D}}$$

For the case when $20 > A + D > 10$, a correction factor of $|A + D| - 1$ is applied. The significance of change cannot be obtained from the above formula when $A + D < 10$.

In Table A2:4, the diagonal represents 'no change'; area D represents 'favourable change'; and area A represents 'unfavourable change'.

Table A2:4

No change	Before: 7	6	5	4	3	2	1
After: 7				Area D =			
6					Favourable change		
5					(sum the scores in		
4	Area A =				this area)		
3		Unfavourable change					
2		(sum the scores in					
1			this area)				

No change

In the hypothetical example above we observe that:

D = 71 (favourable change)
A = 16 (unfavourable change)
13 (no change)
100 ← (check sample size)

$$\text{Significance of change } (t) = \frac{|A - D|}{\sqrt{A + D}} = \frac{|16 - 71|}{\sqrt{87}} = \frac{55}{9.33} = 5.88$$

From Table A2:10 we observe that for a sample N of 100* the t value:

1.98 is significant at $p < 0.05$
2.62 $p < 0.01$

We conclude that $t = 5.88$ indicates a highly significant change from the pre-test to the post-test in the direction of 'useful' in the evaluation of the course on memory.

**Note:* Table A2.10 is interpolated at d.f. = 120, the value nearest to $N = 100$.

The Binomial Test (used in Experiment 9).
In Experiment 9 the question was posed: Supposing that out of 25 adjectival pairs, the experimental group change is found to be in a more favourable direction in respect of 20 scales and in a less favourable direction in respect of five. Can one conclude that overall, the change in the experimental group is significantly towards greater favourability? The binomial test enables us to answer this.

Analysis by means of the binomial test

In our hypothetical example, out of 25 adjectival pairs (the number of cases we have observed), five are in the direction of less favourable.

1   Enter Table A2:5 at 25 in the vertical column on the left-hand side of the table and at 5 in the horizontal column across the top of the table.
2   Double the figure located at the intersection of 25 with 5 (i.e. 0.002 x 2 = 0.004) (see glossary p. 236 for one-tailed and two-tailed tests).

3   0.004 is the probability that with respect to the experimental group results 20 favourable and five unfavourable changes could have occurred by chance.

4   The chances of such an occurrence are only four in 1,000 times. Therefore we must conclude that 996 times out of 1,000 the change towards favourability did not occur by chance but as a result of some other factor – in our hypothetical example, probably as a result of the experimental approach to the teaching of the psychology of memory.

Table A2:5 The Binomial Test

Table of Probabilities Associated With Values As Small As Observed Values of x

N \ x	0	1	2	3	4	5	6	7	8	9	10	11	12	13	14	15
5	031	188	500	812	969	†										
6	016	109	344	656	891	984	†									
7	008	062	227	500	773	938	992	†								
8	004	035	145	363	637	855	965	996	†							
9	002	020	090	254	500	746	910	980	998	†						
10	001	011	055	172	377	623	828	945	989	999	†					
11		006	033	113	274	500	726	887	967	994	†	†				
12		003	019	073	194	387	613	806	927	981	997	†	†			
13		002	011	046	133	291	500	709	867	954	989	998	†	†		
14		001	006	029	090	212	395	605	788	910	971	994	999	†	†	
15			004	018	059	151	304	500	696	849	941	982	996	†	†	†
16			002	011	038	105	227	402	598	773	895	962	989	998	999	†
17			001	006	025	072	166	315	500	685	834	928	975	994	996	†
18			001	004	015	048	119	240	407	593	760	881	952	985	990	999
19				002	010	032	084	180	324	500	676	820	916	968	979	998
20				001	006	021	058	132	252	412	588	748	868	942	961	994
21				001	004	013	039	095	192	332	500	668	808	905	933	987
22					002	008	026	067	143	262	416	584	738	857	895	974
23					001	005	017	047	105	202	339	500	661	798	846	953
24					001	003	011	032	076	154	271	419	581	729	788	924
25						002	007	022	054	115	212	345	500	655		885

From: Non-Parametric Statistics by S. S. Siegel, (c), 1956. McGraw-Hill Book Company Inc. (Reproduced by permission.)

A Significance Test for the difference between two observed proportions (used in Experiment 5).
(Reproduced by kind permission of Professor J. Brown, and *Occupational Psychology*, 1956, 30, pp. 169 to 174).

In Experiment 5 the distribution of responses of sandwich course students and student teachers in respect of the use of coercive power was:

Table A2:6 Coercive Power (Supervisors' ability to punish)

Target group	n	Very important	Quite important	Not very important	Not important at all
Sandwich students	78	1	3	34	40
Student teachers	91	0	1	52	38

The distribution of responses in the two groups being compared does not permit the use of chi-square as a means of analysis. It is possible, however, to determine whether or not a significantly greater proportion of sandwich course students than student teachers record the view that their supervisors' coercive power is 'not very important' or 'not important at all'.

Let us suppose that we are interested in such a comparison in respect of the response 'not important at all'. Data from the two frequency distributions are set out below:

Sandwich Course Students   Student Teachers

(No. in sample) $n_1 = 78$ (No. in sample) $n_2 = 91$

(Frequency in cell 'not important at all') $f_1 = 40$ (Frequency in cell 'not important at all') $f_2 = 38$

(Proportion) $p_1 = \dfrac{f_1}{n_1} = 0.513$ (Proportion) $p_2 = \dfrac{f_2}{n_2} = 0.417$

For the Brown test for the significance of the difference between two observed proportions we need the following information:

d = the difference between the proportions
    (i.e. $p_1 - p_2 = 0.513 - 0.417 = 0.096$)
N = the total sample (i.e. $n_1 - n_2 = 169$)
$Nd^2 = 169 \times (0.096)^2 = 0.155$

R = the ratio of the two groups $= \dfrac{n_2}{n_1}$

(the samples are labelled so that $n_2 > n_1$)

$$= \frac{91}{78} = 1.15 \quad (1.2 \text{ corrected to 1 decimal place})$$

$$p = \frac{f_1 + f_2}{N} = \frac{40 + 38}{169} = 0.46$$

Having determined that:

$$Nd^2 = 0.155$$
$$R = 1.2$$
$$p = 0.46,$$

we can now enter Tables A2:7 or A2:8, pp. 218 and 219.

In Table A2:7 expressing Nd^2 values required for significance at the 5 per cent level, the value of Nd^2 when $R = 1$ (the nearest to $R = 1.2$ in our example) and when p = 0.5 (the nearest to $p = 0.46$ in our example) is $Nd^2 = 3.84$.

Our observed value for Nd^2 (0.155) is very much less than the required value. We conclude that sandwich course students as compared with student teachers do not differ in the degree to which they record the use of coercive power by their respective supervisors as 'not important at all'.

Further Applications

Where the researcher needs to examine a large number of percentage differences it may prove useful to employ a technique which does not require calculations from raw data. Treatment 14 (p. 220) illustrates the use of nomographs in testing the statistical significance of differences between percentages.

Table A2:7 Table Values of Nd^2 required for significance at the 5 per cent level

R \ p	0.500	0.600 / 0.400	0.650 / 0.350	0.700 / 0.300	0.725 / 0.275	0.750 / 0.250	0.775 / 0.225
1.0	3.84	3.69	3.50	3.23	3.06	2.88	2.68
1.5	4.00	3.84	3.64	3.36	3.19	3.00	2.79
2.0	4.32	4.15	3.93	3.63	3.45	3.24	3.01
2.5	4.71	4.52	4.28	3.95	3.75	3.53	3.28
3.0	5.12	4.92	4.66	4.30	4.08	3.84	3.57
3.5	5.56	5.33	5.06	4.67	4.43	4.17	3.88
4.0	6.00	5.76	5.46	5.04	4.79	4.50	4.19
4.5	6.46	6.20	5.87	5.42	5.15	4.84	4.50
5.0	6.91	6.64	6.29	5.81	5.51	5.19	4.82
6.0	7.84	7.53	7.14	6.59	6.25	5.88	5.47
8.0	9.72	9.33	8.85	8.17	7.75	7.29	6.78
10.0	11.6	11.2	10.6	9.76	9.27	8.72	8.11
12.0	13.5	13.0	12.3	11.4	10.8	10.1	9.43
14.0	15.4	14.8	14.0	13.0	12.3	11.6	10.8
16.0	17.3	16.7	15.8	14.6	13.8	13.0	12.1
20.0	21.2	20.3	19.3	17.8	16.9	15.9	14.8

From: *Occupational Psychology*, 30, pp. 169–174, 1956 (Reproduced by permission).

| 0.800 | 0.825 | 0.850 | 0.875 | 0.900 | 0.920 | 0.935 | 0.950 |
0.200	0.175	0.150	0.125	0.100	0.080	0.065	0.050
2.46	2.22	1.96	1.68	1.38	1.13	0.934	0.730
2.56	2.31	2.04	1.75	1.44	1.18	0.973	0.760
2.77	2.50	2.20	1.89	1.56	1.27	1.05	0.821
3.01	2.72	2.40	2.06	1.69	1.39	1.14	0.894
3.28	2.96	2.61	2.24	1.84	1.51	1.25	0.973
3.56	3.21	2.83	2.43	2.00	1.63	1.35	1.06
3.84	3.47	3.06	2.63	2.16	1.77	1.46	1.14
4.13	3.73	3.29	2.82	2.32	1.90	1.57	1.23
4.43	3.99	3.53	3.03	2.49	2.03	1.68	1.31
5.02	4.52	4.00	3.43	2.82	2.31	1.91	1.49
6.22	5.62	4.96	4.25	3.50	2.86	2.36	1.85
7.44	6.71	5.93	5.08	4.18	3.42	2.82	2.21
8.66	7.81	6.90	5.92	4.87	3.98	3.29	2.57
9.88	8.91	7.87	6.75	5.56	4.54	3.75	2.93
11.1	10.0	8.85	7.59	6.24	5.11	4.22	3.30
13.6	12.2	10.8	9.26	7.62	6.23	5.15	4.02

Table A2:8 Table Values of Nd^2 required for significance at the 1 per cent level

p R	0.500 0.400	0.600 0.350	0.650 0.300	0.700 0.275	0.725 0.250	0.750 0.225	0.775
1.0	6.63	6.37	6.04	5.57	5.29	4.98	4.63
1.5	6.91	6.63	6.29	5.81	5.51	5.18	4.82
2.0	7.46	7.17	6.79	6.27	5.95	5.60	5.21
2.5	8.13	7.80	7.40	6.83	6.48	6.10	5.67
3.0	8.85	8.49	8.05	7.43	7.06	6.63	6.17
3.5	9.60	9.21	8.73	8.06	7.65	7.20	6.69
4.0	10.4	9.95	9.43	8.71	8.27	7.78	7.23
4.5	11.1	10.7	10.1	9.37	8.89	8.36	7.78
5.0	11.9	11.5	10.9	10.0	9.52	8.96	8.33
6.0	13.5	13.0	12.3	11.4	10.8	10.2	9.45
8.0	16.8	16.1	15.3	14.1	13.4	12.6	11.7
10.0	20.1	19.3	18.3	16.9	16.0	15.1	14.0
12.0	23.4	22.4	21.3	19.6	18.6	17.5	16.3
14.0	26.7	25.6	24.3	22.4	21.3	20.0	18.6
16.0	30.0	28.8	27.3	25.2	23.9	22.5	20.9
20.0	36.6	35.1	33.3	30.7	29.2	27.4	25.5

From: *Occupational Psychology*, 30, pp. 169—174, 1956 (Reproduced by permission).

| 0.800 | 0.825 | 0.850 | 0.875 | 0.900 | 0.920 | 0.935 | 0.950 |
0.200	0.175	0.150	0.125	0.100	0.080	0.065	0.050
4.25	3.83	3.38	2.90	2.39	1.95	1.61	1.26
4.42	3.99	3.52	3.02	2.49	2.03	1.68	1.31
4.78	4.31	3.81	3.27	2.69	2.20	1.81	1.42
5.20	4.69	4.15	3.56	2.93	2.39	1.98	1.54
5.66	5.11	4.51	3.87	3.18	2.60	2.15	1.68
6.14	5.54	4.89	4.20	3.45	2.82	2.33	1.82
6.63	5.99	5.29	4.54	3.73	3.05	2.52	1.97
7.14	6.44	5.69	4.88	4.01	3.28	2.71	2.12
7.64	6.90	6.09	5.22	4.30	3.52	2.90	2.27
8.67	7.82	6.91	5.93	4.88	3.99	3.29	2.57
10.7	9.70	8.57	7.35	6.05	4.94	4.08	3.19
12.8	11.6	10.2	8.78	7.23	5.91	4.88	3.81
15.0	13.5	11.9	10.2	8.41	6.88	5.68	4.44
17.1	15.4	13.6	11.7	9.60	7.85	6.48	5.07
19.2	17.3	15.3	13.1	10.8	8.82	7.28	5.69
23.4	21.1	18.7	16.0	13.1	10.8	8.89	6.95

Testing the statistical significance of differences between percentages by the use of nomographs (used in Experiment 5).

Nomographs offer a quick and simple way of inspecting the differences between percentages for statistical significance. All that is necessary is a ruler (a transparent one is best) by which to read the charts. We read all three nomographs included below in the same way, i.e. by placing the ruler at our two percentage values on the left- and right-hand side of the chart respectively and then reading off the value on the middle line. Figure A2:1 gives us a significant value, a value which is dependent upon the sizes of our respective samples. The significant value is that value which must be reached or exceeded on nomograph Figures A2:2, A2:3 is the difference between the two percentages being compared is to be accepted as statistically significant. By way of example, if we use the data from Treatment 13 (p. 216) to do with our sandwich course students and student teachers, we place the ruler at the point 78 in the left-hand column (the sample size of sandwich course students) and 91 in the right-hand column (the sample size of student teachers). The ruler intersects the middle line of Figure A2:1 at a value of 0.154 (approximately).

On Figure A2:2 we compare our observed percentages in respect of our sandwich course and student teachers, that is 51 per cent (0.513 corrected to two decimal places) in the left-hand column, and 42 per cent (0.417 corrected to two decimal places) in the right-hand column. Placing the ruler on these two values, the point of intersection on the middle line is at (approximately) 0.09 at the 0.05 level of significance. The obtained value 0.09 falls short of the significant value of 0.154 which must be reached or exceeded for statistical significance and we conclude that there is no significant difference between the sandwich course students and student teachers, a finding, incidentally, which corroborates our calculations in Treatment 13.

Finally, turning to Figure A2:3, note how our obtained value drops to (approximately) 0.065 at the 0.01 level of significance and to (approximately) 0.050 at the 0.001 level of significance in respect of our two percentages being compared.

Figure A2:1

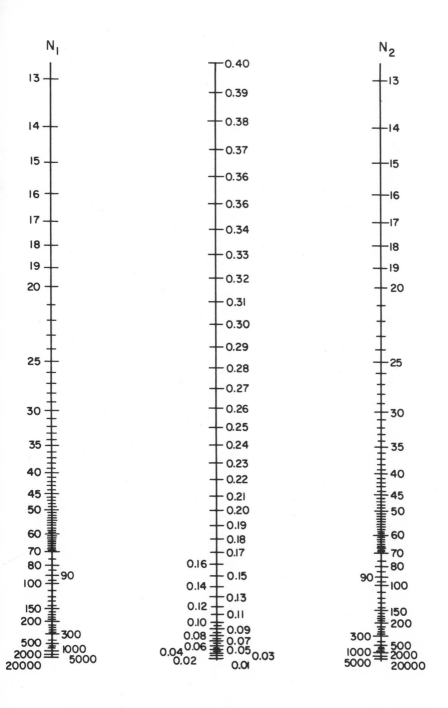

224

Figure A2:2

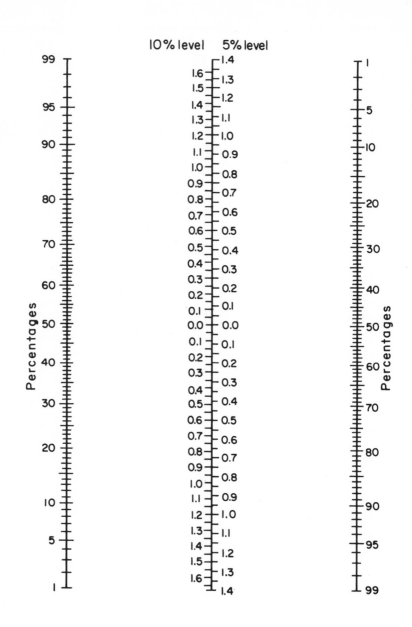

Figure A2:3

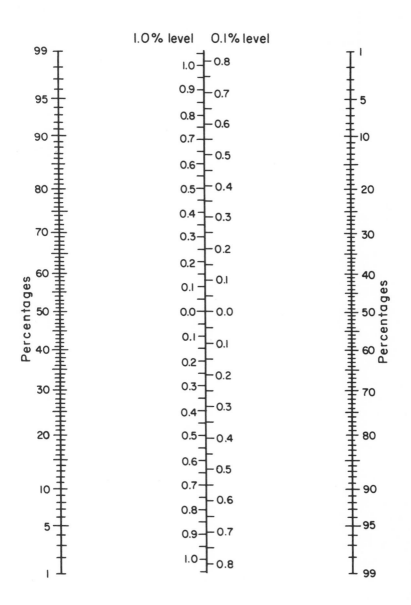

The Median Test

In Experiment 8 the question was posed: 'Do future teachers rank the terminal value "a comfortable life" significantly more highly than future social workers?' The median test is an appropriate technique by which to determine whether or not two independent groups differ in central tendencies. That is to say, whether or not (in our example) future teachers differ from future social workers in the median ratings they attach to a particular value.

The first step in performing the median test is to ascertain the median score for the combined sample of future teachers and future social workers in respect of the value 'a comfortable life'. This was given on p. 73 as 13.71 (see Treatment 2 for computing the median from raw scores).

The second step is to dichotomize the combined set of scores at the combined median (13.71) and to cast our data in a 2 x 2 table as below:

Table A2:9

	Future teachers (n_1)	Future social workers (n_2)	
Scores below combined median	A	B	A + B
Scores above combined median	C	D	C + D
	A + C	B + D	$N = n_1 + n_2$

Where the combined sample is *less* than 20 then a test known as the Fisher Exact Probability Test should be used. This is a useful technique based upon the 2 x 2 table and employed when the two samples are small. (See Siegel, S., *Nonparametric Statistics for the Behavioral Sciences*, McGraw-Hill Book Company Inc., 1956, pp. 96—104, for a full account.)

Where the combined sample is *larger than 40** as in our present example, use chi-square corrected for continuity as in the formula below:

$$\chi^2 = \frac{N\left(|AD - BC| - \dfrac{N}{2}\right)^2}{(A + B)(C + D)(A + C)(B + D)}$$

*Where the combined sample is between 20 and 40, and provided no cell has an expected frequency (See Treatment 7) of less than 5, then χ^2 corrected for continuity may also be employed. Should there be an expected frequency less than five, the Fisher Exact Probability Test should be used.

Our data from Experiment 8, cast in a 2 x 2 table, are:

	Future teachers	Future social workers	
Scores below combined median	A 40	B 11	A + B 51
Scores above combined median	C 21	D 20	C + D 41
	A + C 61	B + D 31	N = 92

$$\chi^2 = \frac{N\left(|AD - BC| - \frac{N}{2}\right)^2}{(A + B)(C + D)(A + C)(B + D)}$$

$$\chi^2 = \frac{92(|800 - 231| - 46)^2}{51 \times 41 \times 61 \times 31} = 6.36$$

$$\chi^2 = 6.36 \quad \text{d.f.} = 1 \quad p < 0.05$$

We conclude that in our example, future teachers rank the terminal value 'a comfortable life' significantly more highly than future social workers.

Table A2:10 Values of t at the 0.05, and 0.01 Levels of Significance

Degree of freedom	Two-tailed test		One-tailed test	
	0.05 level	0.01 level	0.05 level	0.01 lev
1	12.706	63.657	6.314	31.821
2	4.303	9.925	2.920	6.965
3	3.182	5.841	2.353	4.541
4	2.776	4.604	2.132	3.747
5	2.571	4.032	2.015	3.365
6	2.447	3.707	1.943	3.143
7	2.365	3.499	1.895	2.998
8	2.306	3.355	1.860	2.896
9	2.262	3.250	1.833	2.821
10	2.238	3.169	1.812	2.764
11	2.201	3.106	1.796	2.718
12	2.179	3.055	1.782	2.681
13	2.160	3.012	1.771	2.650
14	2.145	2.977	1.761	2.624
15	2.131	2.947	1.753	2.602
16	2.120	2.921	1.746	2.583
17	2.110	2.898	1.740	2.567
18	2.101	2.878	1.734	2.552
19	2.093	2.861	1.729	2.539
20	2.086	2.845	1.725	2.528
21	2.080	2.831	1.721	2.518
22	2.074	2.819	1.717	2.508
23	2.069	2.807	1.714	2.500
24	2.064	2.797	1.711	2.492
25	2.060	2.787	1.708	2.485
26	2.056	2.779	1.706	2.479
27	2.052	2.771	1.703	2.473
28	2.048	2.763	1.701	2.467
29	2.045	2.756	1.699	2.462
30	2.042	2.750	1.697	2.457
40	2.021	2.704	1.011	1.352
60	2.000	2.660	1.000	1.330
120	1.980	2.617	0.990	1.309
∞	1.960	2.576	0.980	1.288

Adapted from Kellaway (1968)

Table A2:11 Value of F required for 0.05 level of significance

Denominator df = number of scores minus the number of sub-groups
Numerator df = (number of sub-groups $-$ 1)

	1	2	3	4	5	6	7
1	4052.2	4999.5	5403.4	5624.6	5763.6	5859.0	5928.4
2	98.50	99.00	99.17	99.25	99.30	99.33	99.36
3	34.12	30.82	29.46	28.71	28.24	27.91	27.67
4	21.20	18.00	16.69	15.98	15.52	15.21	14.98
5	16.26	13.27	12.06	11.39	10.97	10.67	10.46
6	13.75	10.92	9.78	9.15	8.75	8.47	8.26
7	12.25	9.55	8.45	7.85	7.46	7.19	6.99
8	11.26	8.65	7.59	7.01	6.63	6.37	6.18
9	10.56	8.02	6.99	6.42	6.06	5.80	5.61
10	10.04	7.56	6.55	5.99	5.64	5.39	5.20
11	9.65	7.21	6.22	5.67	5.32	5.07	4.89
12	9.33	6.93	5.95	5.41	5.06	4.82	4.64
13	9.07	6.70	5.74	5.21	4.86	4.62	4.44
14	8.86	6.51	5.56	5.04	4.69	4.46	4.28
15	8.68	6.36	5.42	4.89	4.56	4.32	4.14
16	8.53	6.23	5.29	4.77	4.44	4.20	4.03
17	8.40	6.11	5.18	4.67	4.34	4.10	3.93
18	8.29	6.01	5.09	4.58	4.25	4.01	3.84
19	8.18	5.93	5.01	4.50	4.17	3.94	3.77
20	8.10	5.85	4.94	4.43	4.10	3.87	3.70
21	8.02	5.78	4.87	4.37	4.04	3.81	3.64
22	7.95	5.72	4.82	4.31	3.99	3.76	3.59
23	7.88	5.66	4.76	4.26	3.94	3.71	3.54
24	7.82	5.61	4.72	4.22	3.90	3.67	3.50
25	7.77	5.57	4.68	4.18	3.85	3.63	3.46
26	7.72	5.53	4.64	4.14	3.82	3.59	3.42
27	7.68	5.49	4.60	4.11	3.78	3.56	3.39
28	7.64	5.45	4.57	4.07	3.75	3.53	3.36
29	7.60	5.42	4.54	4.04	3.73	3.50	3.33
30	7.56	5.39	4.51	4.02	3.70	3.47	3.30
40	7.31	5.18	4.31	3.83	3.51	3.29	3.12
60	7.08	4.98	4.13	3.65	3.34	3.12	2.95
120	6.85	4.79	3.95	3.48	3.17	2.96	2.79
∞	6.63	4.61	3.78	3.32	3.02	2.80	2.64

Adapted from Kellaway (1968)

8	9	10	12	15	20	24	∞
5881.1	6022.5	6055.8	6106.3	6157.3	6208.7	6234.6	6260.6
99.37	99.39	99.40	99.42	99.43	99.45	99.46	99.47
27.49	27.35	27.23	27.05	26.87	26.69	26.60	26.50
14.80	14.66	14.55	14.37	14.20	14.02	13.93	13.84
10.29	10.16	10.05	9.89	9.72	9.55	9.47	9.38
8.10	7.98	7.87	7.72	7.56	7.40	7.31	7.23
6.84	6.72	6.62	6.47	6.31	6.16	6.07	5.99
6.03	5.91	5.81	5.67	5.52	5.36	5.28	5.20
5.47	5.35	5.26	5.11	4.96	4.81	4.73	4.65
5.06	4.94	4.85	4.71	4.56	4.41	4.33	4.25
4.74	4.63	4.54	4.40	4.25	4.10	4.02	3.94
4.50	4.39	4.30	4.16	4.01	3.86	3.78	3.70
4.30	4.19	4.10	3.96	3.82	3.66	3.59	3.51
4.14	4.03	3.94	3.80	3.66	3.51	3.43	3.35
4.00	3.89	3.80	3.67	3.52	3.37	3.29	3.21
3.89	3.78	3.69	3.55	3.41	3.26	3.18	3.10
3.79	3.68	3.59	3.46	3.31	3.16	3.08	3.00
3.71	3.60	3.51	3.37	3.23	3.08	3.00	2.92
3.63	3.52	3.43	3.30	3.15	3.00	2.92	2.84
3.56	3.46	3.37	3.23	3.09	2.94	2.86	2.78
3.51	3.40	3.31	3.17	3.03	2.88	2.80	2.72
3.45	3.35	3.26	3.12	2.98	2.83	2.75	2.67
3.41	3.30	3.21	3.07	2.93	2.78	2.70	2.62
3.36	3.26	3.17	3.03	2.89	2.74	2.66	2.58
3.32	3.22	3.13	2.99	2.85	2.70	2.62	2.54
3.29	3.18	3.09	2.96	2.81	2.66	2.58	2.50
3.26	3.15	3.06	2.93	2.78	2.63	2.55	2.47
3.23	3.12	3.03	2.90	2.75	2.60	2.52	2.44
3.20	3.09	3.00	2.87	2.73	2.57	2.49	2.41
3.17	3.07	2.98	2.84	2.70	2.55	2.47	2.39
2.99	2.89	2.80	2.66	2.52	2.37	2.29	2.20
2.82	2.72	2.63	2.50	2.35	2.20	2.12	2.03
2.66	2.56	2.47	2.34	2.19	2.03	1.95	1.85
2.51	2.41	2.32	2.18	2.04	1.88	1.79	1.70

Table A2:12 Value of F required for 0.01 level of significance

Denominator df = number of scores minus the number of sub-groups
Numerator df = (number of sub-groups − 1)

	1	2	3	4	5	6	7
1	161.45	199.50	215.71	224.58	230.16	233.99	236.77
2	18.51	19.00	19.16	19.25	19.30	19.33	19.35
3	10.13	9.55	9.28	9.12	19.01	8.94	8.89
4	7.71	6.94	6.59	6.39	6.26	6.16	6.09
5	6.61	5.79	5.41	5.19	5.05	4.95	4.88
6	5.99	5.14	4.76	4.53	4.39	4.28	4.21
7	5.59	4.74	4.35	4.12	3.97	3.87	3.79
8	5.32	4.46	4.07	3.84	3.69	3.58	3.50
9	5.12	4.26	3.86	3.63	3.48	3.37	3.29
10	4.96	4.10	3.71	3.48	3.33	3.22	3.14
11	4.84	3.98	3.59	3.36	3.20	3.09	3.01
12	4.75	3.89	3.49	3.26	3.11	3.00	2.91
13	4.67	3.81	3.41	3.18	3.03	2.92	2.83
14	4.60	3.74	3.34	3.11	2.96	2.85	2.76
15	4.54	3.68	3.29	3.06	2.90	2.79	2.71
16	4.49	3.63	3.24	3.01	2.85	2.74	2.66
17	4.45	3.59	3.20	2.96	2.81	2.70	2.61
18	4.41	3.55	3.16	2.93	2.77	2.66	2.58
19	4.38	3.52	3.13	2.90	2.74	2.63	2.54
20	4.35	3.49	3.10	2.87	2.71	2.60	2.51
21	4.32	3.47	3.07	2.84	2.68	2.57	2.49
22	4.30	3.44	3.05	2.82	2.66	2.55	2.46
23	4.28	3.42	3.03	2.80	2.64	2.53	2.44
24	4.26	3.40	3.01	2.78	2.62	2.51	2.42
25	4.24	3.39	2.99	2.76	2.60	2.49	2.40
26	4.23	3.37	2.98	2.74	2.59	2.47	2.39
27	4.21	3.35	2.96	2.73	2.57	2.46	2.37
28	4.20	3.34	2.95	2.71	2.56	2.45	2.36
29	4.18	3.33	2.93	2.70	2.55	2.43	2.35
30	4.17	3.32	2.92	2.69	2.53	2.42	2.33
40	4.08	3.23	2.84	2.61	2.45	2.34	2.25
60	4.00	3.15	2.76	2.53	2.37	2.25	2.17
120	3.92	3.07	2.68	2.45	2.29	2.18	2.09
∞	3.84	3.00	2.60	2.37	2.21	2.10	2.01

Adapted from Kellaway (1968)

8	9	10	12	15	20	24	∞
238.88	240.54	241.88	243.91	245.95	248.01	249.05	250.10
19.37	19.38	19.40	19.41	19.43	19.45	19.45	19.46
8.85	8.81	8.79	8.74	8.70	8.66	8.64	8.62
6.04	6.00	5.96	5.91	5.86	5.80	5.77	5.75
4.82	4.77	4.74	4.68	4.62	4.56	4.53	4.50
4.15	4.10	4.06	4.00	3.94	3.87	3.84	3.81
3.73	3.68	3.64	3.57	3.51	3.44	3.41	3.38
3.44	3.39	3.35	3.28	3.22	3.15	3.12	3.08
3.23	3.18	3.14	3.07	3.01	2.94	2.90	2.86
3.07	3.02	2.98	2.91	2.84	2.77	2.74	2.70
2.95	2.90	2.85	2.79	2.72	2.65	2.61	2.57
2.85	2.80	2.75	2.69	2.62	2.54	2.51	2.47
2.77	2.71	2.67	2.60	2.53	2.46	2.42	2.38
2.70	2.65	2.60	2.53	2.46	2.39	2.35	2.31
2.64	2.59	2.54	2.48	2.40	2.33	2.29	2.25
2.59	2.54	2.49	2.42	2.35	2.28	2.24	2.19
2.55	2.49	2.45	2.38	2.31	2.23	2.19	2.15
2.51	2.46	2.41	2.34	2.27	2.19	2.15	2.11
2.48	2.42	2.38	2.31	2.23	2.16	2.11	2.07
2.45	2.39	2.35	2.28	2.20	2.12	2.08	2.04
2.42	2.37	2.32	2.25	2.18	2.10	2.05	2.01
2.40	2.34	2.30	2.23	2.15	2.07	2.03	1.98
2.37	2.32	2.27	2.20	2.13	2.05	2.01	1.96
2.36	2.30	2.25	2.18	2.11	2.03	1.98	1.94
2.34	2.28	2.24	2.16	2.09	2.01	1.96	1.92
2.32	2.27	2.22	2.15	2.07	1.99	1.95	1.90
2.31	2.25	2.20	2.13	2.06	1.97	1.93	1.88
2.29	2.24	2.19	2.12	2.04	1.96	1.91	1.87
2.28	2.22	2.18	2.10	2.03	1.94	1.90	1.85
2.27	2.21	2.16	2.09	2.01	1.93	1.89	1.84
2.18	2.12	2.08	2.00	1.92	1.84	1.79	1.74
2.10	2.04	1.99	1.92	1.84	1.75	1.70	1.65
2.02	1.96	1.91	1.83	1.75	1.66	1.61	1.55
1.94	1.88	1.83	1.75	1.67	1.57	1.52	1.46

Table A2:13

χ^2 distribution

	0.05	0.01
1	3.84	6.63
2	5.99	9.21
3	7.81	11.34
4	9.49	13.28
5	11.07	15.09
6	12.59	16.81
7	14.07	18.48
8	15.51	20.09
9	16.92	21.67
10	18.31	23.21
11	19.68	24.72
12	21.03	26.22
13	22.36	27.69
14	23.68	29.14
15	25.00	30.58
16	26.30	32.00
17	27.59	33.41
18	28.87	34.81
19	30.14	36.19
20	31.41	37.57
21	32.67	38.93
22	33.92	40.29
23	35.17	41.64
24	36.42	42.98
25	37.65	44.31
26	38.89	45.64
27	40.11	46.96
28	41.34	48.28
29	42.56	49.59
30	43.77	50.89
40	55.76	63.69
50	67.50	76.15
60	79.08	88.38
70	90.53	100.43
80	101.88	112.33
90	113.15	124.12
100	124.34	135.81

Adapted from Kellaway (1968)

Table A2:14 Values of Spearman's Rank Order Correlation Coefficient at Selected Significance Points

	Significance level (one-tailed test	
N	0.05	0.01
4	1.000	
5	0.900	1.000
6	0.829	0.943
7	0.714	0.893
8	0.643	0.833
9	0.600	0.783
10	0.564	0.746
12	0.506	0.712
14	0.456	0.645
16	0.425	0.601
18	0.399	0.564
20	0.377	0.534
22	0.359	0.508
24	0.343	0.485
26	0.329	0.465
28	0.317	0.448
30	0.306	0.432

From: SIEGEL, S. S. (c) (1956)
Non-Parametric Statistics. McGraw-Hill B Company Inc. (Reproduced by permission

GLOSSARY OF TERMS

In the analysis sections of the experiments and in the subsequent description of the statistical treatments for data, the reader will have encountered numerous technical terms and signs. Perplexing though they may appear to the layman, they generally have succinct meanings which economize on language in the description of the results.

The following glossary includes all the terms which readers will have encountered in this text together with some description or definition of those terms.

Cell	The intersection of a row and column in a two-variable table, or more generally the intersection of n variables in an n variable table.
Cognitive Style	A subject's preferred mode of learning, thinking or problem solving.
Control Group	A group of subjects as similar as possible to the experimental group and treated in exactly the same way except that they are not given the experimental treatment. The control group provides a base line against which the effects of this treatment may be measured.
Dependent Variable	That feature of the experimental situation which is not directly under the control of the experimenter. It may be seen as the 'effect' of experimental manipulation.
Dogmatism	Closed-mindedness, high resistance to change.
Experimental Group	The group receiving the experimental treatment.
Factor Analysis	A technique for identifying common characteristics of a number of variables.
Frequency Distribution	An array of values, ranging from the highest to the lowest, together with a report of the number of times each value occurs.
Hypothesis	A tentative and untested assertion about some natural phenomenon.
Independent Variable	That feature of the experimental situation which is systematically manipulated by the experimenter. It may been seen as the 'cause' of the phenomenon under investigation.
Normal Distribution	A symmetrical bell-shaped curve formed around the mean when the frequency distribution of a variable is plotted graphically; and occurring when the variation around that mean is subject to change.

Norm	When used in a sociological context this refers to a generally accepted standard, or value, within a group.
Null Hypothesis	The hypothesis that the experiment has had no significant effect on the dependent variable.
One-Tailed/ Two-Tailed Tests	In a situation where the experimenter has predicted the direction of the difference between the means of two samples a one-tailed test is appropriate. Where the experimenter is concerned only to show that there is a difference between the means of two samples, a two-tailed test is appropriate.
Parameter	Some characteristic of a population, e.g. the mean, median or standard deviation.
Population (Or Universe)	The entire group of subjects or observations which fall within the category being observed.
Pre-Test/Post-Test	Estimates of behaviour made prior/subsequent to experimental manipulation.
Random Assignment	A means of choosing a sample from a population in such a way that each member has an equal chance of selection.
Representative Sample	A sample, drawn from a population, which accurately reflects all the characteristics of that population.
Role Conflict	Tension arising from simultaneous and conflicting demands upon the individual.
Sample	A portion of a total population that is taken as representative of the entire population.
Skewness	The extent to which the frequency curve is asymmetrical because of an unequal division of cases on either side of the mode.
Standard Deviation	The standard deviation is a measure of the spread, or dispersion, of the scores about the mean.
Statistically Significant	The result of an experiment is said to be statistically significant if it can be shown that it is highly unlikely to have occurred just by 'chance'. Usually if the odds against 'chance' are more than 20:1 (i.e. a probability of less than 0.05) the result is accepted as statistically significant.
Stereotype	Distorted classifications of people or events based on oversimplification.

ALLEN V. L., Situational Factors in Conformity, in Berkowitz L. (Ed.), *Advances in Experimental Social Psychology*, Academic Press, New York, 1965, **2**, pp 133—175.

ALLPORT G. W. & POSTMAN L. J., The Basic Psychology of Rumour, in Maccoby E. E., Newcomb T. M. and Hartley E. L. (Eds.) *Readings in Social Psychology*, Methuen, London, 1961.

ANDERSON B. & JOHNSON W., Two Kinds of Set in Problem Solving, *Psychological Reports*, 19, pp. 851—858, 1966.

ANDREAS, B. G. Experimental Psychology. John Wiley, New York, 1960.

ANNETT J., Feedback and Human Behaviour, Penguin, London, 1969.

ANNETT M., The Classification of Instances of Four Common Class Concepts, *British Journal of Educational Psychology*, 29, pp. 223—236, 1959.

ASPIN D., On the 'Educated' Person and the Problem of Values in Teacher Education and Training, in Lomax D., (Ed.) *The Education of Teachers in Britain*, John Wiley, London, 1973.

ATKINSON R. C. & SHIFFRIN R. M., Human Memory: A Proposed System and its Control Processes, in Spence K. & Spence J. (Eds.) *The Psychology of Learning and Motivation: Advances in Research and Theory*, **2**, Academic Press, New York, 1968.

ATKINSON R. C. & SHIFFRIN R. M., The Control of Short-term Memory, *Scientific American*, August 1971, pp. 82—90, 1971.

AUSUBEL D. P. & BLAKE E., Proactive Inhibition in the Forgetting of Meaningful School Material, *Journal of Educational Research*, 54, pp. 145—149, 1958.

BADDELEY A. D., Human Memory in Dodwell P. C. (Ed.) *New Horizons in Psychology* **2** Penguin, London, 1972.

BAKER C. H. & YOUNG P., Feedback during Training and Retention of Motor Skills, *Canadian Journal of Psychology*, **14**, pp. 257—264, 1960.

BARTLETT F. C., Remembering, Cambridge University Press, 1932.

BERG I. A. & BASS B. M., (Eds.), *Conformity and Deviation*, Harper & Row, New York, 1961.

BLAU P. M. & SCOTT W. R., *Formal Organizations: A Comparative Approach*, Routledge & Kegan Paul, London, 1963

BLOMMERS P. & LINDQUIST E. F., *Elementary Statistical Methods in Psychology and Education*, University of London Press, 1960.

BOLTON C. D. & KAMMEYER C. W., *The University Student: A Study of Student Behavior and Values*, College and University Press, New Haven, Connecticut, 1967.

BORGER R. & SEABORNE E. M., The Psychology of Learning, Pelican, London, 1966.

BOUSFIELD W. A., The Occurrence of Clustering in the Recall of Randomly Arranged Associates, *Journal of General Psychology*, 49, pp. 229—240, 1953.

BROWN G., SHAW M. & TAYLOR S., An Experiment to Examine the Use of Four Common Class Concepts by Primary School Children, *Papers in Education*, No. 1, *Journal of Anstey College*, 1969.

BROWN J., A Modified Significance Test for the Difference Between Two Observed Proportions, *Occupational Psychology*, 30, pp. 169—174, 1956.

BROWN R. W., Social Psychology, Free Press, New York, 1965.

BUTCHER H. J., Human Intelligence, Methuen University Press, 1970.

BYRNE D. & WONG T. J., Racial Prejudice, Interpersonal Attraction and Assumed Dissimilarity of Attitudes, *Journal of Abnormal and Social Psychology*, 65, pp. 246—253, 1962.

CENTERS R., The Psychology of Social Classes, Russell & Russell, New York, 1961.

CERASO J., The Interference Theory of Forgetting, *Scientific American*, October 1967, pp. 117—124, Reprint No. 509, 1967.

CHAMBERS E. G., Statistical Calculations for Beginners, Cambridge University Press, 1964.

CHILD D., Psychology and the Teacher, Holt, Rinehart & Winston, London, 1973.

COHEN L., Functional Dependence, Exchanges and Power of Influence, *International Journal of Educational Sciences*, **3**, 1, pp. 47—51, 1969.

COHEN L., Students' Perceptions of the School Practice Period, *Research in Education*, 2, pp. 52—58, 1969.

COHEN L., Sixth Form Pupils and Their Views of Higher Education, *Journal of Curriculum Studies*, **2**, 1, pp. 67—72, 1970.

COHEN L., Anxiety, Ambiguity and Supervisory Style in Relation to Students' Evaluation of Their Thin Sandwich Course Experience, *Bulletin of Mechanical Engineering Education*, 10, pp. 297—302, 1971.

COHEN L., Personality and Problems in a College of Education Environment, *Durham Research Review*, **6**, 28, pp. 617—622, 1972(a).

COHEN L., School to College: Some Initial Problems of Adjustment Among First-Year Student Teachers. *Education for Development*, **2**, 2, pp. 3—9, 1972(b).

COHEN L., REID I. & BOOTHROYD K., Validation of the Mehrabian Need for Achievement Scale with College of Education Students, *British Journal of Educational Psychology*, **43**, 3, 1973.

COHEN L. & SCAIFE R., Self-Environment Similarity and Satisfaction in a College of Education, *Human Relations*, **26**, 1, 1973.

COHEN L. & TOOMEY D., Role Orientations and Subcultures among Undergraduate Students: an Empirical Investigation in a Technological University, *Research in Education*, 1973.

CONNOLLY T. G. & SLUCKIN W., Statistics for the Social Sciences, Cleaver Hume, London, 1962.

CORCORAN D. W. J., The Relation between Introversion and Salivation *American Journal of Psychology*, **77**, 2, pp. 298—300, 1964.

CRAIK F. I. M., Primary Memory, *British Medical Bulletin*, **27**, pp. 323—326, 1971.

CRONBACH L. J., Essentials of Psychological Testing, Harper & Row, New York, 1960.

DANZIGER K., Socialization, Penguin, London, 1971.

DAVIS R., SUTHERLAND N. S. & JUDD B., Information Content in Recognition and Recall, *Journal of Experimental Psychology*, 61, pp. 422—428, 1961.

DEAN D. G. & VALDES D. M., Experiments in Sociology, Appleton—Century—Crofts, New York, 1963.

DEESE J., The Psychology of Learning, McGraw-Hill Book Company Inc., New York, 1957.

DEESE J. & KAUFMAN R. A., Serial Effects in Recall of Unorganized and Sequentially Organized Verbal Material, *Journal of Experimental Psychology*, 54, pp. 180—187, 1957.

EDWARDS A. L., Statistical Methods for the Behavioral Sciences, Holt, Rinehart & Winston, New York, 1967.

ENTWISTLE N. J., Personality and Academic Attainment, *British Journal of Educational Psychology*, **42**, 2, pp. 137—151, 1972.

ENTWISTLE N. J. & NISBET J., Educational Research in Action, University of London Press, 1972.

ETZIONI A., Modern Organizations, Prentice—Hall, New York, 1964.

EYSENCK H. J., The Psychology of Politics, Routledge & Kegan Paul, London, 1954.

EYSENCK H. J., Sense and Nonsense in Psychology, Penguin, London, 1957.

EYSENCK H. J., Race, Intelligence and Education, Temple Smith, London, 1971.

EYSENCK H. J. & EYSENCK S. B. G., Eysenck Personality Inventory, Educational and Industrial Testing Service, 1964.

EYSENCK H. J. & EYSENCK S. B. G., On the Unitary Nature of Extraversion, *Acta Psychologica*, 26, pp. 383—390, 1967.

FEATHER N. T., Educational Choice and Student Attitudes in Relation to Terminal and Instrumental Values. *Australian Journal of Psychology*, **22**, 2, pp. 127—143, 1970.

FEATHER N. T., Value systems and Education: The Flinders programme of Value Research, *The Australian Journal of Education*, **16**, 2, pp. 136—149, 1972.

FELDMAN K. A., Studying the Impacts of Colleges on Students, *Sociology of Education*, **42**, 3, pp. 207—237.

FINLAYSON D. S. & COHEN L., The Teacher's role: A Comparative Study of the Conceptions of College of Education Students and Head Teachers, *British Journal of Educational Psychology*, **37**, 1, pp. 22—31, 1967.

FRENCH J. R. P. & RAVEN B. H., The Bases of Social Power, In D. Cartwright (Ed.) *Studies in Social Power*, Ann Arbor, University of Michigan Press, Michigan, 1959.

GETZELS W., Conflict and Role Behavior in the Educational Setting, In W. W. Charters and N. L. Gage (Eds.) *Readings in the Social Psychology of Education*, Allyn & Bacon, New York, 1963.

GLANZER M. & CUNITZ A. R., Two Storage Mechanisms in Free Recall, *Journal of Verbal Learning and Verbal Behaviour*, 5, pp. 351—360, 1966.

GLASS G. V. & STANLEY J. C., Statistical Methods in Education & Psychology, Prentice—Hall, New York, 1970.

GUILFORD J. P., Fundamental Statistics in Psychology & Education, McGraw-Hill Book Company Inc., Maidenhead, 1965.

HART J. T., Second-Try Recall, Recognition and the Memory-Monitoring Process, *Journal of Educational Psychology*, 58, pp. 193—197, 1967.

HAYS W. L., *Statistics* Holt, Rinehart & Winston, New York, 1969.

HILL W. F., *Learning: A Survey of Psychological Interpretations*, Methuen, London, 1964.

HOLDING D. H., *The Principles of Training*, Pergamon Press, Oxford, 1965.

HOWE M. J. A., *Introduction to Human Memory*, Harper & Row, New York, 1970.

HULL C. L., The Goal Gradient Hypothesis and Maze Learning, *Psychological Review*, 39, pp. 25—43, 1932.

HULL C. L., *Principles of Behavior*, Appleton—Century—Crofts, New York, 1943.

HUMPHREY G. & ARGYLE M., *Social Psychology Through Experiment*, Methuen, London, 1962.

HUNTER I. M. L., The Influence of Mental Set on Problem Solving, *British Journal of Psychology*, 47, 63—64, 1956.

HUNTER I. M. L., The Solving of Five-Letter Anagram Problems, *British Journal of Psychology*, 50, 193—206, 1959.

HUNTER I. M. L., *Memory*, Penguin, London, 1964.

JOHNSON D. M., *The Psychology of Thought and Judgement*, Harper & Row, New York, 1955.

KAGAN J., *Understanding Children: Behavior, Motives, and Thought*, Harcourt, Brace and Jovanovich, New York, 1971.

KAGAN J., MOSS H. A. & SIGEL I. E., Psychological Significance of Styles of Thinking, in J. C. Wright & J. Kagan (Eds.) Basic Cognitive Processes in Children, *Monograph of Society for Research in Child Development*, **28**, 2, pp. 73—112, 1963.

KAHN R. L. WOLFE D. M. QUINN R. P. SNOEK J. D. and ROSENTHAL R. A., *Organizational Stress: Studies in Role Conflict and Ambiguity*, John Wiley, New York, 1964.

KELLAWAY F. W., (Ed.) *Penguin—Honeywell Book of Tables*, Penguin, London, 1966.

KELSALL R. K. & KELSALL H. M., *The School Teacher in England and the United States*, Pergamon Press, Oxford, 1969.

KELVIN P., *The Bases of Social Behaviour*, Holt, Rinehart & Winston, London, 1969.

KERLINGER F. N., *Foundation of Behavioral Research*, Holt, Rinehart & Winston, London, 1970.

KRAMER E., Judgement of Personal Characteristics and Emotions from Non-Verbal Properties of Speech, *Psychological Bulletin*. 60, pp. 408—420, 1962.

LEVINE J. M. & MURPHY G., The Learning and Forgetting of Controversial Material, *Journal of Abnormal and Social Psychology*, 38, pp. 507—517, 1943.

LEWIS D. G., *Statistical Methods in Education*. University of London Press, 1967.

LINDGREN H. C., BYRNE D. & PETRINOVITCH L., *Psychology: an Introduction to Behavioral Science*, John Wiley, New York, 1961.

LUCHINS A. S., Classroom experiments on mental set, *American Journal of Psychology*, 59, pp. 295—298, 1946.

MANNION L., An Investigation into the Process of Teacher Socialization. PhD dissertation, School of Research in Education, University of Bradford, 1974.

McGEOCH J. A., Meaningful Relation and Retroactive Inhibition, *American Journal of Psychology*, 43, pp. 579—588, 1931.

McLEISH J., *Students' Attitudes and College Environments*, Institute of Education, Cambridge, 1970.

McNULTY J. A., An Analysis of Recall and Recognition Processes in Verbal Learning, *Journal of Verbal Learning and Verbal Behaviour*, 4, pp. 430—436, 1965.

MILLER G. A., The Magical Number Seven, Plus or Minus Two: Some Limits on our Capacity for Processing Information, *Psychological Review*, 63, pp. 81—97.

MORONEY M. J., *Facts from Figures*, Pelican, London, 1951.

NATIONAL OPINION POLL Nos 109, 110, June 1972.

NESBITT J. E., *Chi-Square*, Manchester University Press, 1966.

NORMAN D. A., *Memory and Attention*, John Wiley, New York, 1969.

OPPENHEIM A. N., *Questionnaire Design and Attitude Measurement*, Heinemann, London, 1966.

OSGOOD C. E., TANNENBAUM P. H. & SUCI G. J., *The Measurement of Meaning*, University of Illinois, Urbana, 1957.

PHILLIPS J. L., *The Origins of Intellect: Piaget's Theory*, Freeman, San Francisco, 1969.

POSTMAN L. & RAU L., Retention as a Function of the Method of Measurement, *University of California Publications in Psychology*, 8, pp. 217—270, 1957.

REID I. & COHEN L., Achievement Orientation, Intellectual Achievement Responsibility, and Choice Between Degree and Certificate Courses in Colleges of Education, *British Journal of Educational Psychology*, **43**, 1, 1973.

REID I. & COHEN L., Male and Female Achievement Orientation and Intellectual Responsibility: A British Validation Study, *Educational and Psychological Measurement*, 34, pp. 379-382, 1974.

RICHARDSON K. & SPEAR D., (Ed.) *Race, Culture & Intelligence*, Penguin, London, 1972.

ROBSON C., *Experimental Design and Statistics in Psychology*, Penguin, London, 1973.

ROKEACH M., *The Open and Closed Mind*, Basic Books, New York, 1960.

ROKEACH M., *Beliefs, Attitudes and Values*, Josse Bass, San Francisco, 1968.

ROKEACH M., Value Systems in Religion, *Review of Religious Research*, 11, pp. 3—23, 1969.

ROKEACH M., *The Nature of Human Values*, Free Press Macmillan, New York, 1973.

ROKEACH M., MILLER M. & SNYDER J. A., The Value Gap between Police and Policed, *Journal of Social Issues*, 27, 2, pp. 155—171, 1971.

ROSENBERG M., *Occupations and Values*, The Free Press, Glencoe, Illinois, 1957.

SECORD P. F., BEVAN W. & DUKES W. F., Occupational and Physiognomic Stereotypes in the Perception of Photographs, *Journal of Social Psychology*, 37, pp. 261—270, 1953.

SIEGEL S. S., *Non-Parametric Statistics.* McGraw-Hill Book Company Inc., New York, 1956.

SKINNER B. F., An Operant Analysis of Problem Solving in Kleinmuntz B., (Ed.) *Problem Solving Research, Method and Theory*, Wiley, New York, 1966.

SLAMECKA N. J. & CERASO J., Retroactive and Proactive Inhibition of Verbal Learning, *Psychological Bulletin*, 57, pp. 449—475, 1960.

START K. B. The Success of a Group of Teachers in Relation to their Personal and Professional Background, Unpublished PhD thesis, University of Manchester, 1966.

STEVENS S. S., (Ed.), *Handbook of Experimental Psychology*, Wiley, New York, 1951.

STONES E., *An Introduction to Educational Psychology*, Methuen, London, 1966.

STONES E. & HESLOP J. R., The Formation and Extension of Class Concepts in Primary Schoolchildren, *British Journal of Educational Psychology*, 38, pp. 261—271, 1968.

TAJFEL H. & WILKES A. L., Saliance of Attributes and Commitment to Extreme Judgements in the Perceptions of People, *British Journal of Social and Clinical Psychology* 2, pp. 40—49, 1963.

TAJFEL H., Social and Cultural Factors in Perception in Lindzey G. and Aronson E., (Eds.), *Handbook of Social Psychology*, Vol. 3, Addison—Wesley, Reading, Mass., 1969.

TAJFEL H., Cognitive Aspects of Prejudice, *Journal of Biosocial Science Supplement*, 1, pp. 173—191, 1969.

THORNDIKE E. L., The Law of Effect, *American Journal of Psychology*, 39, pp. 212—222, 1927.

THORNDIKE E. L., *The Fundamentals of Learning*, New York Teachers' College, Columbia University, 1932.

TOLMAN E. C., *Purposeful Behavior in Animals and Men*, Appleton—Century—Crofts, New York, 1932.

TULVING E., Subjective Organization in Free Recall of 'Unrelated Words', *Psychological Review*, 69, pp. 344—354, 1962.

VENESS T. & BRIERLY D. W., Forming Impressions of Personality: Two Experiments, *British Journal of Social and Clinical Psychology*, 2, pp. 11—19, 1963.

WOODWORTH R. S. & SCHLOSBERG H., *Experimental Psychology*, Methuen, London, 1966 edition.

DETAILS OF EXPERIMENTAL PROCEDURES
FOR EACH EXPERIMENT

EXPERIMENT No. 1

This experiment requires pairs of observers to record certain specific aspects of motorists' behaviour. It is essential to discuss thoroughly with all observers the suggestions made on p. 16 for the systematic recording of the observed behaviour.

EXPERIMENT No. 2

Do *not* turn to p. 19 to read any details of the experiment until told to do so.

When the instructor distributes cards to each member of the group, please cooperate to ensure the success of the experiment *by not reading any card other than your own.*

This experiment requires a group of seven to ten
subjects. If you have been selected you should now
leave the room and decide amongst yourselves the
order in which you will re-enter. Upon re-entry you
will be given your instructions.

If you have not been selected as a subject you will
act as a scorer.

Do *not* turn to p. 29 until told to do so by the
instructor.

Scorers (and subjects when they have completed
their task) should turn to page 29 in section 2 for
full details of the aims, procedures and analyses of
this study.

Do *not* turn to p. 39 of the experiment until told to do so.

Please complete the following information about yourself.

Male   Female

Main subjects

Please write in the number of 'A level' GCEs you have* obtained at each particular grade.

*If a sixth former, please give a *frank* and *honest* assessment of your likely performance in your forthcoming 'A-level' examinations.

Please do *not* turn to p. 47 until told to do so by the instructor

EXPERIMENT No. 6

Please do *not* turn to p. 54 to read any details of the experiment until told to do so by the instructor

Self-identities and Behaviour in Organizations

Before turning over to continue the study of self-identities in organizations would you kindly supply the following information about yourself and your activities

Do *not* write your name anywhere on the page. The information you give should be *absolutely anonymous*

Male ☐ Female ☐

Please put a number in the appropriate boxes below to indicate how many 'A' level passes you obtained and at what grades.

E	D	C	B	A	If none please tick here
☐	☐	☐	☐	☐	☐

Approximately how many hours per week do you spend in private study?

☐	☐	☐	☐	☐	☐
0–3	4–7	8–11	12–15	16–19	20 or more

How great a degree of 'clash' do you experience between the study requirements of your course(s) and your social activities?

☐	☐	☐	☐	☐	☐
None at all	Some	A fair amount	A con-siderable amount	A great degree	An enormous amount

What proportion of people who share your spare-time activities are your fellow students?

None at all	Some	A fair number	A considerable number	A great number	All

Where do you live?

At home	Alone in digs	In digs with other students	In a hall of residence

Do *not* write in the boxes below

SI	SF	V	R	A

SF	AI	V	R

This experiment requires samples of three or more
different occupational groups, or, in the case of
students, *intending-occupational groups.*
It is important to complete the first values questionnaire (p. 90) before going on to score the second
(p. 91)

Male

Female

Age

18—23   24—29   30—35.   over 35

OCCUPATION (IF ALREADY QUALIFIED) OR INTENDING OCCUPATION

(please write in)

VALUING:
a study of students' attitudes towards a section of
their course

Do *not* read any section of the experiment on p. 99
until told to do so by the instructor

You will be told that you belong either to group 1 or group 2. Do *not* ask the significance of this, it will become clear later in the experiment. Follow the instructions given by the experimenter and do *not* consult the section on p. 108 until you are told to do so.

EXPERIMENT No. 11

Everyone in the group performs this experiment in the same way. Listen carefully to the instructions given by the experimenter. Do *not* consult the section on p. 113 until you are told to do so.

You will be assigned to one of four groups. Do not ask the significance of this but remember the group to which you belong. Do *not* consult the section on p. 117 until the experimenter tells you that the testing is over.

EXPERIMENT No. 13

For this experiment you need a viewing frame. If these have not been provided turn to Appendix 1b p. 185 for details of how to construct one. You will be assigned to one of three groups for this experiment. Do *not* ask the significance of this, it will become clear later. Follow the experimenter's instructions carefully and turn to the section on p. 121 when told to do so.

All subjects perform this task in the same way. All you will require is a pen or pencil, test papers will be provided. Listen carefully to the instructions. Further details are on p. 127 but do *not* refer to these until told to do so.

EXPERIMENT No. 15

You will be told to select a partner for this experiment — each pair will consist of one subject and one experimenter. Follow the instructions given by the tutor and do *not* consult the section on p. 135 until you are told to do so.

You will be required to select a partner for this experiment — each pair will consist of one subject and one experimenter. Each pair will be randomly assigned to either group 'E' or group 'C'. Do *not* ask the significance of this, it will become clear later in the experiment. Follow the instructions given by the instructor.

EXPERIMENT No. 17

You will be told to select a partner for this experiment — each pair will consist of one subject and one experimenter. Follow the instructions given by the tutor and do *not* consult the section on p. 143 until you are told to do so.

This experiment is different from the others in this book. It is a simple fieldwork exercise using young children (aged from 5–11 years) as subjects. You may read the whole experimental outline given on p. 151

Do *not* write your name anywhere on the page.
The information you give should be *anonymous*.

Male   Female

Please put a number in the appropriate boxes below
to indicate how many 'A' level passes you obtained
and at what grades.

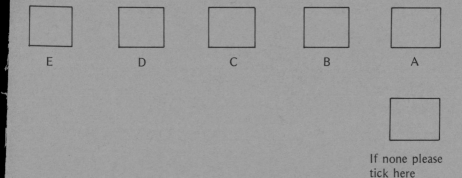

E   D   C   B   A

If none please
tick here

Turn to p. 161 when told to do so.

Take a piece of paper from the envelope. Place it on
your moist tongue and count silently to twenty.
Remove the paper and dispose of it. *Do not taste it
again, or take another piece.*

Record the taste of the paper by putting a tick in
the appropriate box:

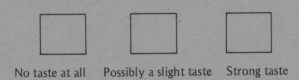

No taste at all   Possibly a slight taste   Strong taste

Now turn to p. 173 for further details.

EXPERIMENT No. 21

You will be required to select a partner for this
experiment — each pair will consist of one subject
and one experimenter. Follow the instructions given
by the tutor and do *not* consult the section on p. 175
until you are told to do so.